THE

PLACE OF

IMMUNITY

THE PLACE OF IMMUNITY

Revised 1996

© 1994 Francis Frangipane
ISBN 1-886296-14-6
Printed in the United States of America

Sixth Printing, February 1998

Arrow Publications
P.O. Box 10102
Cedar Rapids, IA 52410-0102
Phone: (319) 373-3011
Fax: (319) 373-3012

PREFACE

This book is the first of a two-volume set dealing with the theme of God's protection. The second book is called *The Divine Antidote* and, among other things, attends to the specifics of protecting oneself from curses and the effects of witchcraft.

At one point these two books were united under a single cover. However, prior to publishing we felt that, though similar in content, each book had enough distinctions in style and subject matter to exist as companion books.

It is our prayer that *The Place of Immunity* and *The Divine Antidote* will not only be companions to each other but to the reader as well. And, by the grace of the Lord Jesus, may they hew out of our hearts an abode for the living Presence of God.

CONTENTS

INTRODUCTION

The Bible tells us of a time when Satan shall be cast down to the earth. He will come, "**having great wrath, knowing that he has only a short time**" (Rev. 12:12). While some Christians question whether the church shall be the victim of such hellish warfare, it is obvious even in our world today that the magnitude of evil has escalated.

What is our response? Has God provided for us a Christian equivalent to the ark He provided Noah? Is there a spiritual Goshen where we can dwell in safety during God's judgments? We believe the answer to these questions is "Yes." God has provided spiritual protection for Christians, a Place of Immunity where our souls can always find safe harbor.

When we speak of immunity, we do not mean we will escape suffering, persecution or even death for Jesus' sake. For "**all who desire to live godly in Christ Jesus will be persecuted**" (2 Tim. 3:12). Nor do we expect to find a place where we are so "spiritual" that the world finally loves us. For if they hated Jesus, they will hate us as well (John 15:18–19). The Place of Immunity is the shelter of God; it is that dwelling of eternal life the Lord has provided for our souls.

Once we have found this place, nothing we encounter in life can defeat us; God Himself preserves us in all things. In every distress or devilish plot set against us, we emerge the better for it. It is the redemptive power of Christ reversing the plans of Satan and annulling the effects of death in our lives.

Although you may be in a place of fear, sin or emotional defeat, your current condition is not a limitation to the Almighty. From where you are, you can reach the Place of Immunity.

—FRANCIS FRANGIPANE

Kept by God

We know that no one
who is born of God sins;
but He who was born of God
keeps him
and the evil one
does not touch him.

— 1 John 5:18 —

1

WHERE THE DESOLATE FIND GOD

THE GREAT "PRESSURE"

Jesus gave the last hours of this age a poignant headline. He called this period "The Great Tribulation." The word rendered *tribulation* meant "grievous affliction or distress; pressure or burden upon the spirit." As we move closer toward the end of this age, catastrophic distresses and pressures upon man shall increase.

Added to the increasing pressures of our times is the *decreasing* desire of government, school systems and law enforcement to restrain moral decadence. We live in a time when a significant portion of our society is in open and defiant rebellion toward God. The prophetic words of the Second Psalm are being fulfilled before our eyes.

> **Why are the nations in an uproar, and the peoples devising a vain thing? The kings of the earth take their stand, and the rulers take counsel together against the Lord and against His Anointed: 'Let us tear their fetters apart, and cast away their cords from us!' "** —Psalm 2:1–3

With the loss of deterrents, a tidal wave of violence and unrestrained lawlessness has risen, inducing fear and outrage in America. The once familiar structures of respect and order, as though made of sand, are so worn down that they are barely discernible. Even the memory of simpler, more wholesome times fades as our civilization crumbles into social chaos.

If you are one who has stood unyieldingly against the increasing darkness, you know how intense and multifaceted the battle is. Whether you are fighting to heal your city's wounds or warring against abortion and pornography, remedy one evil and it seems ten others storm in.

Christians on the front lines are weary. A number are just going through the motions; still others have stopped fighting altogether. Daniel warned of a time when the enemy would **"wear down the saints of the Highest One"** (Dan. 7:25). To emerge victorious from this day in which we live, we must discover the Place of Immunity prepared for us by God.

ELIJAH: A MAN LIKE US

Elijah was a man with passions like our own and he fought in a spiritual war similar to ours. In his battle for the soul of Israel, he stood against the wiles of Jezebel and

Ahab. Yet, his most intense battle was not against a visible foe but against personal discouragement.

As bold as Elijah was, he lived as a fugitive, moving in and out of places of hiding. Jezebel had murdered nearly all of the Lord's prophets, replacing the godly influence they brought with the dark cloud of satanic oppression that accompanied the priests of Baal and the Asherah.

A new initiative, however, had come from the Lord. Both Elijah and the prophets of Baal were to build altars to the deity they each served. The God who answered with fire would be acknowledged as Lord over the nation. King Ahab and all Israel came to the confrontation.

Try as they may, the priests of Baal could draw no response from their god. But when Elijah prayed, fire immediately fell upon his sacrifice. This was Elijah's greatest victory, and when the Israelites saw the display of God's power, they bowed to the ground saying, **"The Lord, He is God; the Lord, He is God"** (1 Kings 18:39).

But the Lord was not finished. After Elijah had the priests of Baal destroyed, he prayed and the Lord brought rain, ending a terrible three-year drought. On this one day, both fire and rain fell from heaven!

If this tremendous day had occurred at virtually any other time in Israel's history, the nation would have repented, but it did not. Baal worship should have ended, but it continued. In fact, nothing changed. Instead of the revival which Elijah expected, the opposite occurred: An enraged Jezebel vowed to kill Elijah and he fled until he sat exhausted and discouraged beneath a juniper tree in the wilderness. There, the weary prophet prayed, **"It is enough; now, O Lord, take my life, for I am not better than my fathers"** (1 Kings 19:4).

Elijah had offered the Lord his very best effort. Like the prophets before him, Elijah could not bring revival to the northern tribes of Israel. Discouragement overwhelmed him. He had enough.

Have you said, *"It is enough"?* Perhaps you were frustrated by your own inability to truly effect positive change in your family, church or society. Possibly you gave your all but found little success. Disheartened and weary, like Elijah, you wished to die. You said, *"It is enough! I have done all I know to do!"*

With all his natural resources spent, Elijah laid down and slept; as he did, an angel touched him and told him, **"Arise, eat."** At his head were bread and water. Elijah, weary with life itself, ate and withdrew back into sleep. Once more the angel touched him; **"Arise,"** he said, **"eat, because the journey is too great for you"** (v. 7).

For all our visions, plans and programs, God's will cannot be accomplished without His strength. The journey before each of us is also "too great." We need the strength that only comes from the Almighty's touch.

RETURN TO YOUR BEGINNINGS

"So he arose and ate and drank, and went in the strength of that food forty days and forty nights to Horeb, the mountain of God" (v. 8). The Lord gave Elijah strength, not to send him back to battle but to bring him back to basics.

If, in seeking to fulfill the task God has given us, we sacrifice our daily devotional life, our lives will soon become dry and desolate. To restore our souls, the Lord brings us back to the essentials of our faith. He reminds us that our first and highest purpose is not to save our nation but to give Him pleasure. Without this focus, we lose touch with the Presence of God; we are outside the Place of Immunity.

Elijah was led to **"Horeb, the mountain of God."** In Hebrew *Horeb* means "desolation": the barren environment mirrored Elijah's soul.

This was not the first time the Lord guided a servant of His to Horeb. It was here, five centuries earlier, that the Lord appeared in the burning bush to Moses. In his zeal, Moses had tried, but failed, to liberate Israel from Egyptian oppression. He also had fled to Horeb. As a fugitive from Pharaoh, Moses lived forty years in desolation.

When the Lord brought Moses to Horeb, it was for two reasons: to reveal Himself to His servant and to initiate a new beginning based solely upon God's sustaining power. In the eyes of Moses, Horeb had been a time of desolation. To God, however, Horeb was a place where He prepared His servants for new beginnings. As the Lord had met Moses, He now would meet Elijah.

HOW DID YOU GET HERE?

Perhaps Elijah's greatest virtue was his zeal. Indeed, we shall see that twice in his communication with God, Elijah speaks of having been **"very zealous"** for the Lord. But zeal, unattended by wisdom, eventually becomes its own god; it compels us toward expectations which are unrealistic and outside the timing and anointing of God.

To remain balanced, zeal must be reined in and harnessed by strategic encounters with the living God. We otherwise become frustrated with people and discouraged with delays. We step outside our place of strength and spiritual protection.

Elijah had come to Horeb and lodged there in a cave. Soon, the Word of the Lord came to him: **"What are you doing here, Elijah?"** (v. 9) Elijah was a prophet to Israel, which was perhaps 200 miles north.

This is one of the most important questions God can ever ask us: *"What are you doing here?"* In a deeper sense, His question probes the reality of our spiritual state. He is asking, *"How did your service to Me become dry and desolate?"* He wants us to know that, when we fail to esteem Him as our first love, we will always find a desert awaiting us.

Our primary purpose must be to abide in Christ. For we can otherwise become so consumed with the deteriorating condition of the world that we fail to see the deteriorating condition of our own soul. In His love, the Lord stops us and demands we look at our life. *Is this existence which I now live the abundant life promised me from Christ?*

> IT IS A GREAT DECEPTION TO BECOME SO CONSUMED WITH THE DETERIORATING CONDITION OF THE WORLD THAT WE FAIL TO SEE THE DETERIORATING CONDITION OF OUR OWN SOUL.

We can be honest at Horeb. We have nothing to prove and no need to pretend. Here, at Horeb, the internal mechanisms of defensiveness and pride crumble. If we are disappointed, we are free to express it; if frustrated, we can admit it. We must simply and truthfully evaluate, without rationalization, our heart's condition.

In our transparency, the Presence of God draws near our hearts. Is not intimacy with God the very thing we have neglected? And is not the Lord alone our source of strength in battle? If the enemy can distract us from our time alone with God, he will keep us isolated from the power and help that comes from God in overcoming our battles.

Some of us are sincerely striving to accomplish God's will without the companionship of Jesus. Recall the story of Joseph and Mary after the Passover in Jerusalem (Luke 2:41–49). Supposing the child Jesus was with them, they journeyed home. But Jesus was neither with them nor with their relatives; three days later they found Him in the temple.

Likewise, many of us have become so consumed with our battles that we are no longer aware of the Presence of Jesus; we have been traveling in our own strength. Jesus' parents returned to where they had last seen Him, and so also must we. To renew us, God is bringing us back to our most recent encounter with the living Christ. He is bringing us back to basics.

As the pressures and warfare of this age continue to intensify, we realize that yesterday's anointing will not suffice for today's battles. In the next chapter we shall see how, on this sacred mountain, the Lord brought a new beginning to Elijah's life—one that would ultimately release a "double portion" of power to Elijah's servant, Elisha. Under this new anointing, Jezebel would be destroyed and Baal worship abolished!

To reach this same place of breakthrough in our own times, God is bringing us back to the simplicity and purity of devotion to Christ (2 Cor. 11:1–3). What seems like a time of desolation is more truly a time of preparation: *A revival of great proportions is coming to our land!* Here, at your Horeb, God has prepared for you a new beginning. When you return to the battle, you shall war from a Place of Immunity.

Lord Jesus, apart from You my life is dry and desolate. Forgive me for trying to do Your will without abiding in Your Presence. I desperately need You, Lord.

This day, I commit my heart to return to my first love. Teach me, Lord, to consider intimacy with You the greatest measure of my success. Let me see Your glory; reveal to me Your goodness; guide me, O Holy Spirit, into the Presence of Jesus Christ. Amen.

Prisoners
of the Hope

As for you also,
because of the blood
of My covenant with you,
I have set your prisoners free
from the waterless pit.

Return to the stronghold,
O prisoners who have the hope;
This very day I am declaring
that I will restore double to you.

— Zechariah 9:11–12 —

2

THE KNOWLEDGE
OF GOD'S WAYS

TRUE SUCCESS

There are striking parallels between the life of Moses and that of Elijah. Not only did they each appear with Christ on the Mount of Transfiguration, but during their individual lifetimes they both endured an extended time of desolation. Significantly, each found God anew on Mount Horeb. Their similar encounters with the Lord on this holy mountain speak prophetically to all who have not understood their own season of desolation.

Mount Horeb was a place where a desolate soul could again find the Presence of God. It was also a place where the Lord released new assignments and power for His servant's life. The Horeb experience tells us that God accommodates our times of desolation and uses them to prepare us for greater glory.

Therefore, let us return to Moses' second Horeb encounter with God. For it will not only help us understand Elijah's experience with God, it will help us understand our own.

Moses, like Elijah, was frustrated with people. In spite of having recently seen God's hand in deliverance at the Red Sea, Israel returned to idolatry. In anger, Moses shattered the Ten Commandments given him by God and with great passion he reproved Israel.

> MOSES GRASPED THAT THE ONLY WAY ONE COULD TRULY SERVE MAN WAS TO FIRST FIND FULFILLMENT IN GOD.

As angry as he was with God's people, Moses' countenance changed as he ascended Mount Horeb. Perhaps he realized that his only lasting place of peace would be with God.

Accordingly, when Moses drew near to the glory of God, he asked for more than mere victory for Israel in battle; he asked to know the Lord. Moses' greatest achievement would not be his leadership nor deliverance of Israel. His greatest gift to the world would be his example of a life intimately close to God.

He prayed, "If I have found favor in Thy sight, let me know Thy ways, that I may know Thee" (Ex. 33:13). It was at Horeb that the Lord first began to reveal His heart to Moses. To know God is to attain the highest honor given unto men. Yet, we cannot truly know the Almighty if we do not know His ways.

The Bible tells us that God revealed His *acts* to the sons of Israel, but He made known His *ways* to Moses (Ps. 103:7). To know the ways of God is to become knowledgeable of the motives of His heart and intimate with the secrets of God's passions. It is to be amazed at the resolve of His love and compelled to humility by His attraction to the lowly.

Several years ago the Lord revealed to me how embryonic my knowledge of Him was. Late one night His Presence filled my bedroom; I did not need faith to know He was there. Instantly, I was aware of the difference between my religious knowledge about God and actually knowing the person of Jesus Christ as Lord of my life. My knowledge of Him was as a tiny island of incomplete information, a mere dot in an ocean of divine realities. I prayed, *"Lord, I have known of You for many years, but how little I truly know You!"*

Moses asked to see God's glory. Perhaps he wanted to behold the splendor or majesty of the Holy One. It is significant that the Lord unveiled His *goodness* to Moses. God's goodness is the wellspring of His glory; to know God's ways is to become intimate with the myriad expressions of His goodness.

The Lord promised Moses, **"My presence shall go with you, and I will give you rest"** (Ex. 33:14). When God's Presence accompanies our actions, all the energy we once spent worrying and planning is reclaimed and offered back to God in praise and service. To enter God's rest does not imply that we have become *inactive* but that God has become *active*.

Thus, Jesus calls, **"Come to Me, all who are weary and heavy-laden, and I will give you rest"** (Matt. 11:28). How the church today, weary and desperate, needs to return to Jesus and re-enter God's rest! Yoked to Christ, our burdens are transferred to the vastness of His strength and abilities.

He becomes to us an untiring resource for our weakness; He is unfailing wisdom for our ignorance. At the place of rest, Christ becomes a continual life-spring of grace and virtue. We can cease from our anxious labors and, unfettered from our ideas and traditions, serve Him in the unlimited strength of His might.

God has always been more concerned with the condition of our hearts than the activity of our hands. *What we become to Him is far more consequential than all we shall ever do for Him.* He wants our love and companionship. Indeed, the Scriptures tell us that He **"jealously desires the spirit which He has made to dwell in us"** (James 4:5). Thus, if our devotion to our task exceeds our devotion to Him, He will personally hinder our success.

It is out of love that God delivers us from the unanointed momentum of our zeal. He intentionally dries up our vigor. The Lord insists that our success not originate from our strength but from our union with Him. Our time of desolation becomes a tool in His hand to work in us a deeper dependency upon Him. Mount Horeb becomes the very site where, in spite of our sense of failure, God reveals to us His goodness. To be personally restored to God's goodness is what Elijah desperately needed. So it is for us.

THE CAVE OF WITHDRAWAL

The Lord asked Elijah, *"What are you doing here?"*

And he said, "I have been very zealous for the Lord, the God of hosts; for the sons of Israel have forsaken Thy covenant, torn down Thine altars and killed Thy prophets with the sword. And I alone am left; and they seek my life, to take it away."
—1 Kings 19:10

It can be a crushing experience to give your very best and still fall short. Elijah had been discouraged with God's people. Thinking he had failed, he fled Jezebel and begged God to take his life. The Scripture tells us that "**hope deferred makes the heart sick**" (Prov. 13:12). Elijah desperately wanted to see the nation awakened in repentance, but he did not understand the role God would have him play. Perhaps Elijah's main mistake was that he was personally shouldering the burden of Israel's revival. Not knowing his own place, he assumed the place of God.

When the heart becomes sick with disappointment and discouragement, it is easy to lose perspective. We must remember, apart from the cooperating work of the Holy Spirit, no man can truly change another person's heart. Much of Elijah's discouragement came from the false expectations he had placed upon himself.

In his dejection, alone and hurting, Elijah withdrew into a cave on Horeb. For us, self-pity can also become a spiritual cave. It can trap us in a dark hole of loneliness and pain. In this place of isolation we fail to hear the encouragement of God; all we really hear is the echo of our own voice magnifying and distorting our problems.

Calling Elijah out of the cave, the Lord told him, "**Go forth, and stand on the mountain before the Lord**" (v. 11). As Elijah stepped out of the cave's darkness, an awesome event occurred.

The Lord was passing by! And a great and strong wind was rending the mountains and breaking in pieces the rocks before the Lord; but the Lord was not in the wind. And after the wind an earthquake, but the Lord was not in the earthquake. And after the earthquake a fire, but the Lord was not in the

fire; and after the fire a sound of a gentle blowing.
—1 Kings 19:11–12

A NEW REVELATION OF GOD

There are times when the Lord must expand our understanding of His will, actually liberating us from the container of our previous experiences. The Lord was passing by, but He was not in the wind, the earthquake or the fire, all of which were familiar symbols to Elijah. The Lord who *caused* these mighty manifestations was not *in* them.

For Elijah, mighty manifestations had been signs of God's approval. But something new was at hand that required a fresh submission to the living God. A new anointing—a "double portion"—was coming! This new work of God would eventually end the reign of Jezebel and destroy Baal worship. The distinguishing characteristic of this new anointing would not only be seen in supernatural manifestations, but in greater wisdom and compassion.

As the last of the signs ended, we read, **"After the fire a sound of a gentle blowing"** (v. 12). This sound was not the voice of God; it was the *prelude* to God's Presence. Elijah recognized the holy silence and **"wrapped his face in his mantle"** (v. 13), lest he look upon God.

Perhaps it was near this very site that Moses, 500 years earlier, hid when the Lord passed by. Now it was Elijah's turn. Entering this eternal stillness was the Person of God.

SEEING HIM WHO IS UNSEEN

Earthquakes, fires and storms—the signs which accompanied Elijah—are the signs of our times as well. But to enter this new level, we must recognize God's nearness when there are no "earthquakes" or "storms" to capture our attention. He demands we enter a more refined relationship with Him—one that is based on His love and whisper of His word, not merely the issues of our times.

Thus, we must learn to hear the voice of Him who rarely speaks audibly and observe the actions of Him who is otherwise invisible. Elijah would gain the courage to endure Jezebel's wrath the same way Moses faced the rage of Pharaoh: **"He endured, as seeing Him who is unseen"** (Heb. 11:27).

We also endure by *seeing Him* who is invisible. But, before we can truly discern the Presence of God, we must recognize the gentle blowing that *precedes* His Presence. What is this spiritual phenomenon? It is the Holy Spirit subduing the activities of earth in preparation for the Lord's approach.

If we are to attain the power needed at the end of this age, we must learn to detect, without great signs, the still small voice of God. He will not fight for our attention; He must be sought. He will not startle us; He must be perceived. It took no special skill to "discern" the earthquake, the fire or the great storm. But to sense the gentle blowing of God, our other activities must cease. In our world of great pressures and continual distractions, the attention of our hearts must rise to the invisible world of God's Spirit. We must learn to "see" Him who is unseen.

A NEW BEGINNING

In the quieting of Elijah's heart, the Lord appeared. Again the Almighty asked, **"What are you doing here, Elijah?"** (1 Kings 19:13) Elijah repeated his former answer: **"I have been very zealous for the Lord . . . and I alone am left; and they seek my life"** (v. 14). Restoring Elijah's perspective, the Lord assured him there were 7,000 Israelites who had not bowed to Baal.

A new commission was about to come. The Lord told Elijah to anoint Hazael as king over Syria and Jehu as king over Israel. He also was to train Elisha, who would be his successor (1 Kings 19:15–16). At Horeb, God released a "double portion" of spiritual power. Although God gave the anointing to Elijah, it would be Elisha who would walk in it.

Indeed, under this powerful new anointing, Elijah's successor, Elisha, would do twice as many miracles (2 Kings 2:9–14). More than a prophet of judgment, Elisha's works would actually resemble Christ's. Elisha multiplied bread (2 Kings 4:42–44); he captured an enemy's army with kindness; he established peace between Israel and the bands of Aram (2 Kings 6:14–23); he healed Naaman, a Syrian general (2 Kings 5:1–14); and anointed Jehu to destroy Jezebel and Baal worship in Israel (2 Kings 9–10). He also presided over the closest thing to revival the northern ten tribes would ever experience (2 Kings 10:28, 30).

Elijah did not personally bring national restoration. Yet, he did receive a greater understanding of his place in God. His call was to "go before" and prepare the way for greater things to come. Many of us are destroying ourselves trying to bring revival. Perhaps our call is more to *prepare* the ground for that which is coming after us.

Elijah was so successful at "preparing the way," his spiritual anointing was apportioned to John the Baptist as a herald to both Christ's first and His second coming (Mal. 4:5–6; Matt. 17:11). Ultimately, God brought Elijah to heaven in a flaming chariot and a whirlwind, which were familiar manifestations to Elijah's heart.

As this age ends, God's promise to us is that, like Elisha, we too shall receive a "double portion" (Isa. 61:7; John 14:12). What can this mean but that the Lord is going to reveal Himself to us in glories we have never known before. But first He must stop our unanointed activities and the striving of our flesh. He must bring us to the end of our strength and the beginning of His. As we cease trying to take God's place we shall, instead, find our place in Him.

Even though the spirit of Jezebel has been blatantly manifest in our world, its days are numbered. Our task is to be still and know that Christ is God. He shall triumph over all His foes. He will be exalted in all the earth and in Him is the Place of Immunity.

Oh, Master, how easily I fall into dead religious habits and spiritual dullness. Lord, I long to know Your ways, to have eyes that really see and ears that clearly hear. Teach me, Lord Jesus, the intimacies of God. Remove the mystery surrounding Yourself, that I might truly know You.

Forgive me for looking for signs instead of listening for Your voice. Oh, God, how I long to truly know You as Moses did, to abide in Your glory. Restore to Your church the double portion You have promised and guide us into the fulness of Your power. In Jesus' name. Amen.

Protected
from All Evil

I will lift up my eyes to the mountains;
From whence shall my help come?
My help comes from the Lord,
Who made heaven and earth.
He will not allow your foot to slip;
He who keeps you will not slumber.
Behold, He who keeps Israel
Will neither slumber nor sleep.
The Lord is your keeper;

The Lord is your shade on your right hand.
The sun will not smite you by day,
Nor the moon by night.
The Lord will protect you from all evil;
He will keep your soul.
The Lord will guard your going out
And your coming in
From this time forth and forever.

— Psalm 121 —

3

THE SHELTER OF GOD

There is a Place of Immunity for the believer, a spiritual fortress in Christ that protects us from the attacks of the devil. For those who abide in this stronghold of God, the onslaught of the wicked one does not touch them. Here, in this dwelling with the Almighty, we are hidden from the effects of the accuser's tongue; we are sheltered from the assignment of the destroyer.

The dictionary defines *immunity* as "freedom or exemption, as from a penalty, burden, duty or evil." This is how the living God wants His children to walk: in *freedom* from the penalties and burdens of sin, *delivered* from the duties of legalistic religion, *protected* and *triumphant* over the assault of the evil one.

Survey the landscape of the Bible. You will find hundreds of examples of God's loving protection. Every time the Lord pleaded with sinful Israel to return to Him, it was to urge them back to His protection; each time they responded, they were secured again within the Place of Immunity. The Scripture says, **"He shielded them and cared for them, guarding them as the apple of his eye"** (Deut. 32:10 NAB).

A FATHER'S CARE

God is not only our Creator; He is also our Father. As such, it is inconceivable that He would leave His children unprotected. In Matthew 6:8, Jesus says that our Father knows our needs before we ask Him. If we, even in our fallen condition, seek to provide for our children, how much more does God in His perfection seek to shelter and care for His offspring!

Scripture testifies that He has **"granted to us everything pertaining to life and godliness, through the true knowledge of Him who called us by His own glory and excellence"** (2 Peter 1:3). The more we possess a true knowledge of the Almighty, the more accessible His provisions for us become. What has He given us? He has prepared an abiding place for us where all that we need concerning life and godliness is ours. It is a place where every spiritual blessing in the heavenly places belongs to us in Christ (Eph. 1:3).

David knew of this Place of Immunity. He wrote, **"The Lord is my rock and my fortress . . . in whom I take refuge; my shield and . . . my stronghold"** (Ps. 18:2). Again, speaking of those who fear God, David prayed, **"Thou dost hide them in the secret place of Thy presence from the conspiracies of man; Thou dost keep them secretly in a shelter from the strife of tongues"** (Ps. 31:20). And again, **"Thou art my hiding place; Thou dost preserve me from trouble; Thou dost surround me with songs of deliverance"** (Ps. 32:7).

In David's personal life, he knew the living God as a spiritual stronghold and a place of safety from conflict. The king was intimately familiar with this special place in God's Presence. It was here, in the fortress of God, that David's soul was sheltered.

FOR THOSE WHO FOLLOW CHRIST

This Place of Immunity was not just a special provision for prophets and godly kings. From the day of Christ's resurrection, the entrance into the citadel of heaven was opened to all who would follow the Messiah. Discovering this abode, where Christ literally floods us with His life, is not merely the subject of this book, it is the object of our existence!

How shall we find this spiritual place? We simply begin by loving Jesus. He said, **"He who loves Me shall be loved by My Father, and I will love him, and will disclose Myself to him"** (John 14:21). If we persevere in love and obedience, Jesus has promised to progressively reveal Himself to us.

Consider the magnitude of Jesus' promise! He continued, **"If anyone loves Me, he will keep My word; and My Father will love him, and We will come to him, and make Our abode with him"** (John 14:23).

This unfolding revelation of Jesus Christ to our hearts is the path to the abode of God. It is this shelter of the Most High which is the Place of Immunity.

In the following chapters, we will enter various dimensions of spiritual protection. In the sequel to this book, *The Divine Antidote*, we will fortify our souls against the cunning of the evil one, exposing the inroads of witchcraft. And we will chart the power God has for those who are fortressed in

His Presence. For now, if you have given your life to Christ and are sincere in your desire to follow Him, it is enough to know that a Place of Immunity awaits you.

Lord, with the psalmist I cry, "When shall I enter the courts of the living God?" You are our Father; do not hide Yourself from us, Your children! Bring us to Your lap, oh God! Hold us to Your heart; assure us with the fulness of Your Spirit that You, indeed, are near. Thank You, Lord!

THE SHELTER

HE WHO DWELLS IN THE SHELTER
OF THE MOST HIGH
WILL ABIDE IN THE SHADOW OF THE ALMIGHTY.
I WILL SAY TO THE LORD, "MY REFUGE
AND MY FORTRESS, MY GOD, IN WHOM I TRUST!"
FOR IT IS HE WHO DELIVERS YOU
FROM THE SNARE OF THE TRAPPER,
AND FROM THE DEADLY PESTILENCE.
HE WILL COVER YOU WITH HIS PINIONS,
AND UNDER HIS WINGS YOU MAY SEEK REFUGE;
HIS FAITHFULNESS IS A SHIELD AND BULWARK.

YOU WILL NOT BE AFRAID
OF THE TERROR BY NIGHT,
OR OF THE ARROW THAT FLIES BY DAY;
OF THE PESTILENCE THAT STALKS IN DARKNESS,
OR OF THE DESTRUCTION
THAT LAYS WASTE AT NOON.
A THOUSAND MAY FALL AT YOUR SIDE,
AND TEN THOUSAND AT YOUR RIGHT HAND;
BUT IT SHALL NOT APPROACH YOU.

— PSALM 91:1–7 —

4

THE WATCHFULNESS OF GOD

THE GOD WHO KEEPS US

The Lord continually watches our lives. From the moment of our conception to the hour of our death, the Lord guards and guides our earthly journey. The psalmist knew God's watchfulness well. He wrote,

O Lord, Thou hast searched me and known me.
Thou dost know when I sit down and when I rise
up; Thou dost understand my thought from afar.
Thou dost scrutinize my path and my lying down,
and art intimately acquainted with all my ways.
Even before there is a word on my tongue, behold,

> O Lord, Thou dost know it all. Thou hast enclosed
> me behind and before, and laid Thy hand upon me.
> —Psalm 139:1–5

The Lord sees our unspoken thoughts; before we move, He is aware of our motives. He knows everything about us. God has sealed us in the Holy Spirit. From the time we were born again, we were clothed in Christ (Gal. 3:27). We belong to Him. We are His property, bought with the price of His blood. He will not let us go easily. **"A vineyard of wine, sing of it! I, the Lord, am its keeper; I water it every moment. Lest anyone damage it, I guard it night and day"** (Isa. 27:2–3).

Even when we do not sense His Presence, He is watching and working, guiding us to Himself. It was His working in us which brought us to Himself; it remains His work to renew us in His image. This is His highest priority and He guards His work **"night and day."**

Again, the psalmist was resting in his knowledge of God's care when he wrote,

> **I will lift up my eyes to the mountains; from whence shall my help come? My help comes from the Lord, who made heaven and earth. He will not allow your foot to slip; He who keeps you will not slumber. Behold, He who keeps Israel will neither slumber nor sleep.** —Psalm 121:1–4

According to God's word, there is a provision made for us that will even keep one's foot from slipping. That provision is the watchfulness of God, where He hedges our path to the Place of Immunity.

GUARDED IN ALL OUR WAYS

The definition of the word *keep* means "to have and retain in one's control or possession." To be kept by God is to be guarded under His control and secured as His possession.

However, until we are fully renewed in the spirit of our minds, where our minds are absorbed into the mind of Christ (1 Cor. 2:16, Phil. 2:5), our thoughts are not always God's thoughts nor are our ways always His ways. Thus, Jesus prayed that the Father would keep us from the evil one (John 17:15); and, in answer to Christ's prayer, the Father has given His angels charge concerning us, to guard us in all our ways (Ps. 91:11, Heb. 1:13–14).

Yet, we have been blind to the presence and work of our angelic friends. We have been like Elisha's servant, who was more threatened by his circumstances than he was aware of God's provision:

> **Now when the attendant of the man of God had risen early and gone out, behold, an army with horses and chariots was circling the city. And his servant said to him, "Alas, my master! What shall we do?"**
>
> **So he answered, "Do not fear, for those who are with us are more than those who are with them." Then Elisha prayed and said, "O Lord, I pray, open his eyes that he may see." And the Lord opened the servant's eyes, and he saw; and behold, the mountain was full of horses and chariots of fire all around Elisha.**   **—2 Kings 6:15–17**

Just as the angels of God surrounded Elisha, so there are angels guarding you. They were at your side protecting you even before you came to Christ.

There may have been a number of times when, had the angels of the Lord not been assigned to you, you might have suffered an untimely death. Indeed, there were other times, difficult times, when the Lord's angels strengthened you, carrying you through hardship and tragedy. You wondered, *"How did I survive?"* You escaped from Satan's clutches because the Lord assigned His angels to you; they strengthened you in your distress.

There were times when even Jesus needed angelic help. The Scriptures tell us that after the Lord faced severe spiritual warfare in the wilderness, **"Then the devil left Him; and, behold, angels came and began to minister to Him"** (Matt. 4:11). At the end of His life, while sweating blood in fervent prayer, we again read, **"Now an angel from heaven appeared to Him, strengthening Him"** (Luke 22:43).

Wherever Jesus was, the angels of God were always at His side. In His most difficult hour Jesus reminded Peter of the Father's readiness to provide angelic help. He said, **"Or do you think that I cannot appeal to My Father, and He will at once put at My disposal more than twelve legions of angels?"** (Matt. 26:53)

God appointed angels to assist and strengthen Jesus, and He has sent angels to assist and strengthen you. As His angels urged Lot and his family to leave Sodom, so angels are urging God's people today to forsake wickedness. Yes, even as you sit and read these words, there are angels watching over you, guarding you as you enter the Place of Immunity.

Lord Jesus, Your Word tells us that all things are open and laid bare before Your eyes. We also read that Your ears attend to our prayers. Your watchfulness is our comfort and our peace.

Yet, Lord, open our eyes, as You did Elisha's servant's, that we might see You. Open our ears that we might hear You. Grant us the peace that comes from knowing Your daily concern for our lives. Amen.

HE WILL GUARD YOU
IN ALL YOUR WAYS

FOR YOU HAVE MADE THE LORD, MY REFUGE,
EVEN THE MOST HIGH, YOUR DWELLING PLACE.
NO EVIL WILL BEFALL YOU,
NOR WILL ANY PLAGUE COME NEAR YOUR TENT.

FOR HE WILL GIVE HIS ANGELS
CHARGE CONCERNING YOU,
TO GUARD YOU IN ALL YOUR WAYS.
THEY WILL BEAR YOU UP IN THEIR HANDS,
LEST YOU STRIKE YOUR FOOT AGAINST A STONE.
YOU WILL TREAD UPON THE LION AND COBRA,
THE YOUNG LION AND THE SERPENT
YOU WILL TRAMPLE DOWN.

— PSALM 91:9–13 —

5

GUARDED
BY HIS WORD

SAFE IN THE WORD

The primary means through which we are kept and preserved by God is through obedience to His word. In the submission of our will to God, our soul finds protection from evil. Consider the apostle John's words to the young men of the first century church. He said, **"I have written to you, young men, because you are strong, and the word of God abides in you, and you have overcome the evil one"** (1 John 2:14).

Abiding in the Word of God brought spiritual strength to the young men in John's day, enabling them to overcome the evil one. Is this not the reason many of us are defeated by the devil—we do not abide in the Word?

Christ's teaching guides us into the Presence of the Father; it is the Father's Presence that both empowers and protects us. Jesus said,

> My sheep hear My voice, and I know them, and they follow Me; and I give eternal life to them, and they shall never perish; and no one shall snatch them out of My hand. My Father, who has given them to Me, is greater than all; and no one is able to snatch them out of the Father's hand.
> —John 10:27–29

No one is stronger than our heavenly Father. As we follow Christ, He positions us in the palm of God's hand. Here, death cannot seize us. Whatever battles we face, we never face them alone. There is none like our God.

"The eternal God is a dwelling place, and underneath are the everlasting arms; and He drove out the enemy from before you, and said, 'Destroy!' " (Deut. 33:27). Underneath our every step are God's everlasting arms. Thus, when we pass through spiritual conflicts and trials, we are walking on eternal ground, continually kept by the power of Christ's indestructible life (Heb. 7:16). Even when we pass through the shadow of death itself, the powers of death cannot hold us. They are kept at bay by His command.

> For I am convinced that neither death, nor life, nor angels, nor principalities, nor things present, nor things to come, nor powers, nor height, nor depth, nor any other created thing, shall be able to separate us from the love of God, which is in Christ Jesus our Lord.
> —Romans 8:38–39

THOSE WHO NEVER SEE DEATH

The Spirit of God is forever redeeming and transforming all that we encounter, causing each event to work for our spiritual good. Indeed, it has been truly stated that rescue is the constant pattern of God's activity; His final act of encouragement is the resurrection.

Jesus promised, **"Truly, truly, I say to you, if anyone keeps My word he shall never see death"** (John 8:51). The Jews to whom Jesus spoke were offended by this statement. They lacked divine logic and the view of life from eternity; they were ignorant of the resurrection power given every follower of Christ.

However, before we judge them too harshly, let us ask ourselves, *"Are we offended by Christ's promise?"* Given the fact that everyone who followed Jesus in the first century died, are we ashamed of the apparent contradictions of this promise? Do we really believe we shall never see death?

The Jews also were perplexed. They countered, **"Now we know that You have a demon. Abraham died, and the prophets also; and You say, 'If anyone keeps My word, he shall never taste of death' "** (John 8:52). But Jesus did not say His followers would never *taste* death; He said we would never *see* death.

Certainly, there are times when we seem engulfed by sorrow, trapped in an incubator of death itself. Yet, this is a glory of our faith: *Though we die, we do not see death; we see life.* We will taste death, but as Christians we ingest life. Yes, if we keep Christ's word throughout the trial, His promise to us is that we shall **"never see death."** For those who live by every word which comes from the mouth of God, the final outcome of each struggle is not death but life in abundance.

Jesus said,

> But you will be delivered up even by parents and
> brothers and relatives and friends, and they will
> put some of you to death, and you will be hated by
> all on account of My name. Yet not a hair of your
> head will perish.   —Luke 21:16–18

He said we may be put to death, yet not even a hair on our
heads shall perish. Is not death the cessation of life? If death
is due to illness, is it not the progressive diminishing of life?
Yet in Christ, every darkened, shadowy valley into which our
human experience descends is predestined to surface in a
broad field of life. We taste death but do not see it.

David said, **"Though I walk through the valley of the
shadow of death, I fear no evil; for Thou art with me"**
(Ps. 23:4). As frightening as death seems, for those who keep
the Word of the Lord death is no more a barrier than a
shadow. For what dies in us is that which was foreordained
to die—the husk of our old nature. While the death of self is
a daily choice, our new inner nature does not die.

**"Therefore we do not lose heart, but though our outer
man is decaying, yet our inner man is being renewed day
by day"** (2 Cor. 4:16). Yes, in the experience of our own
hearts we have the demonstration of God's resurrection
power, effectual both now and in the future. As we keep
Christ's word, our difficulties always culminate in eternal
life. We join Paul in thanking God, **"Who always leads us
in His triumph in Christ, and manifests through us the
sweet aroma of the knowledge of Him in every place"** (2
Cor. 2:14).

In the many faces of death, in spite of our failures,
sicknesses and difficulties, there remains a Place of Immunity. It is here in our holding fast the Word of Life that the
Lord **"keeps [us] and the evil one does not touch [us]"** (1
John 5:18).

There will be a time when, from the vantage point of heaven, we will review our life's experience. In glorious retrospect we shall see every occasion when destruction stood against us. And, we shall also see that it was here, in these very difficulties, that Christ revealed within us His resurrection power! Though we walked through the valley of the shadow of death, we did not die; rather, we learned to fear no evil. From heaven's view, with awe we will each one day say, *"Truly, I have never seen death."*

Lord, it is true. Even now, I know that You have been with me in every trial and battle. Because of Your redemptive power, I have become stronger in the very conflicts through which Satan meant to weaken me; I have prospered in the very battles through which the devil sought to destroy me!

Truly, You have worked all things for good in my life. And even in the areas where I have yet to understand Your purposes, I entrust those also to You. For I know that, because of Your grace, even what seems to be the finality of death itself shall be transformed, and in all things I shall know only the power of Your resurrection life. Amen.

I Will Be With You

Thus says the Lord,
your Creator, O Jacob,
And He who formed you, O Israel,
"Do not fear, for I have redeemed you;
I have called you by name; you are Mine!

"When you pass through the waters,
I will be with you;
And through the rivers,
they will not overflow you.
When you walk through the fire,
you will not be scorched,
Nor will the flame burn you.

"For I am the Lord your God,
The Holy One of Israel, your Savior."

— Isaiah 43:1–3 —

6

THE TRANSFORMED HEART

The Lord has not promised us a world without hardship, but that in the midst of hardship He will be revealed through us.

CHRIST: THE GREAT I AM

What is God's primary purpose for us? Why were we created? From the beginning of time, God created man with one purpose: to make us in His image according to His likeness.

The Lord has never changed His divine intent toward us. Indeed, Paul tells us that God causes all things in our lives to work toward the good of this one eternal goal (see Rom.

8:28–29). What of the difficulties and tribulations that we encounter in this life? In the scheme of God's plan, troubles and afflictions are upgraded to classroom lessons where we learn to appropriate the nature of Christ. Thus, our difficulties compel us toward God and He compels us toward Christlikeness and change.

Thus, the Lord speaks to each of us His promise,

Do not fear, for I have redeemed you; I have called you by name; you are Mine! When you pass through the waters, I will be with you; and through the rivers, they will not overflow you. When you walk through the fire, you will not be scorched, nor will the flame burn you. For I am the Lord your God, the Holy One of Israel, your Savior.
—Isaiah 43:1–3

While His pledge is a great encouragement, we should be mindful that the Lord did not say He would keep us from the fire or the flood waters, but He would be with us in them. Why does the Lord allow us to pass through conflict in the first place? Because it is here that He trains His sons and daughters in Christlikeness.

Recall the story of Jesus' disciples alone without Him upon a turbulent sea (Matt. 14:22–33). Their boat had been battered by the heaving waves and contrary wind. Jesus, walking on the water, came to them sometime in the early morning. His first words were those of comfort. **"Take courage,"** He said, **"It is I; do not be afraid"** (Matt. 14:27).

It is important to note that Christ's assurance, **"It is I,"** literally translated reads, **"I Am."** This phrase is the divine appellation—the eternal designation of God. While Jesus indeed comes to the aid of His disciples, He also reveals Himself transcendent of time's barriers. As such, He proclaims His availability to *all* His disciples. He is God with us, even to the end of the age!

Thus, Jesus still comes to His disciples' aid, manifesting Himself in the storms of our times, defying what seem to be impossible conditions in order to reach us. He is the master of every human distress; He can help us in every circumstance.

Let us silence the fretting unbelief of our hearts. *Christ is capable, even at this moment, to reach us.* Look through the storm until you sense His Presence, until you hear His confident voice saying, *"Take courage, it is I."*

Yet, Jesus has more on His mind than comforting His disciples. It is one thing to trust Christ to calm the storm around us; it is another matter to leave our security and venture with Him on the water! This very setting of raging wind and sea is the classroom in which the Son of God seeks to perfect His disciples' faith.

Let us affirm the Father's highest purpose for us: Jesus did not come simply to console us but to perfect us! This is exactly where He will take us once we are willing! To behold Christ's goal for us of perfection is to truly gaze into another dimension of God.

We should repent of carrying the image of a Savior who fails to confront our sin or challenge our unbelief, for such is a false image of God. If we are to genuinely know Him, we must accept this truth: *Jesus Christ is irrevocably committed to our complete transformation!*

Of all the disciples, Peter alone responds to the occasion with vision and faith. Putting his hands on the upper plank of the rolling boat's side, Peter peers through the dark night and windblown spray. He calls to Jesus, **"Lord, if it is You, command me to come to You on the water"** (v. 28). There is faith in Peter's voice! Jesus summons His disciple—"Come!"

Peter swings his legs over the edge, dangling them above the swirling sea. With his eyes fixed upon Jesus, he steps out, letting his full weight follow both the downward movement of his feet and the upward reach of his faith. Incredibly, Peter is standing—*and now walking*—on the rolling waves toward Jesus!

In the purest sense, however, Peter did not rest his weight upon the water; he stood upon Christ's word: *"Come!"* Peter trusted that if Jesus told him to do the impossible—even to walk on the water—the power to obey would be inherent within the command.

We know that moments later Peter's faith faltered. He began to sink. But there is something extraordinary to be seen in Christ's response—a view into Christ's actual nature and His ultimate purpose. Jesus did not commend or congratulate Peter. He *rebuked* him! We would have expected praise and encouragement, but none came.

Was Jesus angry? No. The truth is, Jesus Christ is relentlessly given to our perfection. He knows that wherever we settle spiritually will be far short of His provision. He also knows that the more we are transformed into His image, the less vulnerable we are to the evils of this world. Thus, He compels us toward difficulties, for they compel us toward God and God compels us toward change. And it is the transformed heart which finds the Place of Immunity.

Lord Jesus, forgive me for fearing during the storms of life. For too long I have not understood Your commitment to my perfection. I have wanted to be saved without being transformed. I have feared the fulness of becoming Christlike.

Bring forth in me Your faith; help me to not misinterpret Your encouragement toward excellence when I fall short. With all my heart, I want to glorify You with my life. Grant me the grace that, when others see what You have accomplished in me, they, too, shall glorify You! Amen.

HE PRESERVES
THE GODLY

FOR THE LORD GIVES WISDOM;
FROM HIS MOUTH COME KNOWLEDGE
AND UNDERSTANDING.
HE STORES UP SOUND WISDOM
FOR THE UPRIGHT;
HE IS A SHIELD
TO THOSE WHO WALK IN INTEGRITY,
GUARDING THE PATHS OF JUSTICE,
AND HE PRESERVES THE WAY
OF HIS GODLY ONES.

THEN YOU WILL DISCERN
RIGHTEOUSNESS AND JUSTICE
AND EQUITY AND EVERY GOOD COURSE.

FOR WISDOM WILL ENTER YOUR HEART,
AND KNOWLEDGE WILL BE PLEASANT
TO YOUR SOUL;
DISCRETION WILL GUARD YOU,
UNDERSTANDING WILL WATCH OVER YOU,
TO DELIVER YOU FROM THE WAY OF EVIL.

— PROVERBS 2:6–12 —

7

GREATER PURITY, GREATER PROTECTION

When we are young in Christ, God accepts us as babes. There comes a time, however, when He begins to deal with us as sons.

NO SHELTER FOR EVIL

There are certain aspects of our lives that not only exist outside of divine protection, but God Himself seeks to destroy them. We must realize that our carnal nature will find no permanent shelter within the Place of Immunity, nor will demonic strongholds of deceit, fear or lust find divine protection.

To find the shelter of God, we must stand with the Lord against sin and compromise. These things must be destroyed or they will destroy us. The transformation of our souls positions us outside of the devil's reach. It raises us up spiritually to seat us in heavenly places.

Yet, it is one thing to know doctrinally that we are positioned with Christ in heaven (Eph. 1:20; 2:6), quite another thing to spiritually function in that lofty place. To motivate us toward Christlikeness, the Holy Spirit not only instructs us in doctrinal truths, but He also thrusts us into storms of conflict and satanic assault. It is in the midst of this confrontation with hell that He works in us the virtues of heaven.

LED BY THE SPIRIT

Our walk with God progresses from learning lessons to having what we just learned tested. This was the Father's pattern with His Son and it is His pattern with us as well. Let us, therefore, consider Jesus.

Just after Christ was baptized by John, the Father affirmed His sonship. What was the next scene? Jesus was compelled by the Holy Spirit into the wilderness. There, the Scripture tells us, the Son of God was **"tempted by the devil"** (Matt. 4:1).

When we think about being "Spirit-led," we envision miracles, healings and winning the multitudes. But before Jesus was led to do wonders, He was led to do battle—and the war was over the purity of His heart. Jesus was **"led up by the Spirit . . . to be tempted by the devil"** (Matt. 4:1). As much as the Father loved His Son, as perfectly as He knew Him, yet still the Father proved the character of His Son through conflict.

The word *tempted* actually means "tested or proven in adversity." While Jesus was always without sin, He learned obedience through the things which He suffered. Likewise, the Father is not hesitant about allowing the enemy a measured assault against us. He is not worried that we will break. In fact, He desires a certain degree of brokenness before He can use us.

It is in spiritual warfare that what God has taught us is proven. Do you pass the tests of God? There is one answer, one result that guarantees our triumph: to become like Jesus in the midst of our test.

As we said, life consists of learning lessons and passing tests. The integrity of God requires that our learning not be mere head knowledge but that our heart be conformed to Christ. Indeed, before the Lord is through with us, the way of Christ will be more than something we know; it will be something we *instinctively* choose in the midst of temptation or battle. This is where we graduate into the power of God.

Entering the Place of Immunity is the result of a lasting work of God in our lives. Jesus compared the extent of yieldedness in His disciples' hearts to a man who **"dug deep and laid a foundation upon the rock"** (Luke 6:48). It is good that He topples our old nature and tests our newest virtues. For, ultimately, the work which God effects, protects.

Let the storms come. Do not fear the threat of life's fire. God has promised to be with us in our adversity. It is there we attain greater purity and in greater purity is found greater protection.

Lord Jesus, You said that the pure in heart shall see God. Purify me, O Lord. Cleanse me of doublemindedness. Deliver me from selfishness and pride.

Lord, I know that in Your earthly life You only did those things You saw the Father do. Create in me those restraints that crucify my instinctive reactions; release me from the captivity of self-preservation. Deliver me from every pursuit except following You. Establish deep in my life the fire of Your glory. Amen.

A HOUSE
UPON A ROCK

"EVERYONE WHO COMES TO ME,
AND HEARS MY WORDS,
AND ACTS UPON THEM,
I WILL SHOW YOU WHOM HE IS LIKE:
HE IS LIKE A MAN BUILDING A HOUSE,
WHO DUG DEEP
AND LAID A FOUNDATION
UPON THE ROCK;
AND WHEN A FLOOD ROSE,
THE TORRENT BURST AGAINST THAT HOUSE
AND COULD NOT SHAKE IT,
BECAUSE IT HAD BEEN WELL BUILT."

— LUKE 6:47–48 —

8

THE BLOOD COVENANT

In this world where divorce is rampant and contractual agreements readily nullified, the concept of uniting with another person in a lifelong covenant is unfamiliar. Because we are not acquainted with the ramifications of making and keeping a covenant, we fail to utilize the eternal power that is already ours through our covenant relationship with God.

From ancient times, a covenant was the highest form of mutual commitment and unity that any two individuals could express. In the Bible, the word *covenant* means to "fetter together." A covenant bound you for life to your covenant partner. It signified that two people had become one.

Often the participants would pass a sword between themselves to represent that any enemy who attacked one would find both set against him. It was a way of saying, *"My arms will be as your arms. My weapons will be as your weapons."*

Another ceremony that accompanied the making of a covenant consisted of passing a sandal from one to another. This act symbolized each individual's commitment to travel as far as would be needed to stand with his friend. Still another ritual called for the two individuals to sacrifice an animal to God; splitting the sacrifice, each then walked between the halves. From that time on, each covenant partner would consider himself half of the "new person" born of their oath.

Because the covenant was a lifelong pledge and often included one's descendants, it was not made quickly or without formality. Indeed, it was the highest expression of mutual commitment. Whether the covenant union was consummated between friends, a husband and wife, or between God and man, there was no greater expression of one's commitment to another. The covenant was the deepest, most enduring commitment between two souls.

HISTORY OF COVENANTS IN THE BIBLE

The Bible is specifically divided along covenant lines. What we call the Old and New *Testaments* should be translated Old and New *Covenants*. The Scriptures reveal that, at various times in history, the Lord initiated covenants with His servants. Of these, there were seven major covenants, six of which God made with the following Old Testament partners: Noah, Abraham, Isaac, Jacob, Moses and David. The seventh and greatest covenant came in the New Testament between the Father and His Son.

To further understand the nature of God and His covenant relationships with man, let us look at some examples of God's covenants in the Scriptures. In Genesis 6:5, we read that the world had become exceedingly wicked, but one man, Noah, found favor with God. This man became God's partner in a covenant that preserved the human race. The Lord told Noah, **"But I will establish My covenant with you; and you shall enter the ark— you and your sons and your wife, and your sons' wives with you"** (Gen. 6:18).

When the Lord begins to move in covenant power, His partner is but one component in a series of divine initiatives orchestrated by God. Consider Noah: Even before he was preserved through the flood, the Lord had preserved his righteousness in spite of the violence and perversion around him. God then called Noah and commissioned him to build the ark. Noah did not have to invent the ark; God gave him the plans. Noah did not search out and bring in the animals—God brought them in. And after they entered the ark, Scripture says the Lord closed the door behind them.

It was not the ark which protected Noah; it was the covenant he had with God. The covenant supplied everything Noah and his family needed to survive the world's greatest calamity. Indeed, Noah's name means *rest*. Noah never questioned if there would really be a flood or how to build an ark. Noah did not waver in unbelief, wondering whether the entire venture was his idea or God's. When one is in covenant with God, he can cease striving; he can rest from the struggle concerning God's plan for his life.

Such is the power supplied to man through a covenant with God. Again, the covenant provides more than what good people can accomplish by trying to be good; it releases more than what clever church people can attain by their own resourcefulness.

Beyond holding to the faith which God Himself inspired, the success of the covenant purpose does not depend upon man. Indeed, the final goal of the covenant is to provide a sweeping display of divine power which ultimately and perfectly brings glory to God. Thus the promise of God to Noah—*"I will establish my covenant with you"*—is itself the assurance that what God has promised shall certainly come to pass.

Consider Abraham. The God of glory appeared to Abraham while he was still in Mesopotamia. God called and prepared his servant, promising him that he would become the heir of the world and the father of many nations. Abraham believed God, leaving the land of his forefathers to sojourn in Canaan as an alien.

But a time came when the Lord again appeared to His servant. God said, **"Do not fear, Abram, I am a shield to you; your reward shall be very great"** (Gen. 15:1). Abraham engaged in a faith dialogue with God. Abram said, **"O Lord God, what wilt Thou give me, since I am childless"** (Gen. 15:2). God's servant was not expressing doubt but seeking to fulfill his faith.

The Lord responded, **"Now look toward the heavens, and count the stars, if you are able to count them. So shall your descendants be."** The next verse reads, **"Then he believed in the Lord; and He reckoned it to him as righteousness"** (Gen. 15:5–6).

There is a more consequential level of faith available to us, one that goes beyond believing that *someday* God is going to do something important with our lives. It is a faith that realizes God is calling us to significance *now*. This is the type of faith the Lord awakened in Abraham. That night the Creator Himself covenanted with Abraham. God told his servant to bring a heifer, a goat, a ram, a turtledove and a young pigeon. **"Then he brought all these to Him and cut** them in two, and laid each half opposite the other" (Gen. 15:10).

At this point, the Lord told Abraham that the Israelites would be strangers enslaved in a strange land for four hundred years, but that they would return to the land which God had promised Abraham.

And it came about when the sun had set, that it was very dark, and behold, there appeared a smoking oven and a flaming torch which passed between these pieces. On that day the Lord made a covenant with Abram, saying, "To your descendants I have given this land." —Genesis 15:17–18

Christ Himself was the flaming torch which passed between the pieces. The smoking oven and flaming torch were prophetic types of when God would lead Israel back to this land, sheltered under a cloud by day and guided by a fire at night. It is also significant that only the flaming torch passed between the sacrificed animals, indicating that the Lord would keep both His commitment *and* Abraham's!

When a covenant was initiated by God, it contained the Lord's unalterable commitment to supply grace and faith to His human counterpart. Again, we see that the initiative for the covenant came from God. Abraham's faith went from "doctrinal" knowledge of God's purposes to a living response.

The Lord also covenanted with Moses on Mount Sinai (also called "Horeb"). This covenant, however, was not an unequivocal guarantee of divine support. It was a pledge based upon national obedience to God's laws, the Ten Commandments. The Lord's support and empowerment of Israel was conditional, not automatic; it was based upon their obedience.

They put the commandments into a gold-lined chest called the Ark of the Covenant. When Israel went to war, they did so with the Ark of the Covenant before them. *The covenant was the power-source of their armies; God Himself was their ally in battles.* When they crossed the Jordan on their return to Canaan, the Ark of the Covenant rested on the shoulders of the priests; it caused the waters to part so the entire nation could possess their inheritance. The power of Israel was in its covenant with God.

THE NEW COVENANT

The entire covenant process is something initiated, established, confirmed and fulfilled by an act of divine will. The response of God's covenant partner is simply to believe in the integrity of God's promise and obey the covenant conditions.

As Christians, we are a covenant people. The power of redemption in what we describe as "Christian life" is power springing from an eternal covenant. Our relationship with God is a *covenant* relationship through Christ. He is the author and perfecter. He is the source, the guide and the goal of our entire salvation process.

So we see that God is a covenant-making, covenant-keeping God. And, of course, the greatest covenant that was ever initiated, fulfilling all other covenants, is the covenant relationship between the Father and the Son: the Blood Covenant.

The terms of this covenant were profound. If the Son of God would live in perfect sinlessness throughout His life, if He then presented His unblemished life to God in redemptive surrender, from that moment into all eternity God would pardon every soul seeking forgiveness. The Father promised in His covenant agreement with His Son to transfer all of mankind's sins onto the cross of Christ.

Today, we are forgiven not for any other reason than that Jesus kept the covenant conditions. We have access to God and forgiveness of sins through Jesus. Every time Satan seeks to condemn us for our sins or accuse us of our failures, we have only to remember the blood of Christ. For our salvation was never based upon our goodness or our works; the foundation of our faith rests upon what Jesus Christ won for us in His covenant with God the Father.

Let us also recognize and rejoice: God did not covenant with a mere man—one limited in vision and weak in fulfillment. In the New Covenant, *God covenanted with God.*

In Christ, we are children of God. As such, we are **"heirs also, heirs of God and fellow heirs with Christ"** (Rom. 8:17). Just as Noah's family reaped the protection of God through Noah's covenant, so we receive access into the Place of Immunity through Christ. And, as Abraham's descendants enjoyed God's covenant promises with Abraham, so we inherit the blessings of all God's covenant promises made to Jesus.

Every time we see a rainbow in the sky, we are reminded that the Lord is a covenant-keeping God. Each remembrance of Israel, once scattered but now returned to the very land promised by God to Abraham, tells us the Almighty is faithful to His covenant promises.

Because of Jesus, the sandal of divine commitment—God's willingness to come from as far as eternity to be at our side—is given to us. God and His covenant partners are united against evil. Our enemies of sickness, poverty and fear are His enemies. His enemies of sin and Satan are our adversaries as well. The sword has been passed between us; we stand back to back with God against our common foes.

The covenant animal of sacrifice is not a bull or a goat; it is a Lamb. God and man pass through the "halves" of Christ. We unite with God through Christ's humanity; God unites with us through Christ's divinity. In Jesus, God and man become one in covenant power.

How awesome You are. You gave Your life in covenant with God for me. I know no love like Yours, no goodness comparable to You. There is none like You, no, not one. Grant me the courage to live in a covenant relationship with You. Grant me the faith that knows You are on my side against sickness and fear, and that I am on Your side against sin and evil. In the power of Your covenant, I shall know complete victory.

WHEN I SEE THE BLOOD

THEY SHALL TAKE SOME OF THE BLOOD
AND PUT IT ON THE TWO DOORPOSTS
AND ON THE LINTEL OF THE HOUSES IN WHICH THEY EAT IT.

FOR I WILL GO THROUGH THE LAND OF EGYPT
ON THAT NIGHT,
AND WILL STRIKE DOWN ALL THE FIRST-BORN
IN THE LAND OF EGYPT, BOTH MAN AND BEAST;
AND AGAINST ALL THE GODS OF EGYPT
I WILL EXECUTE JUDGMENTS—I AM THE LORD.
AND THE BLOOD SHALL BE A SIGN FOR YOU
ON THE HOUSES WHERE YOU LIVE;
AND WHEN I SEE THE BLOOD I WILL PASS OVER YOU,
AND NO PLAGUE WILL BEFALL YOU TO DESTROY YOU
WHEN I STRIKE THE LAND OF EGYPT.

FOR THE LORD WILL PASS THROUGH
TO SMITE THE EGYPTIANS;
AND WHEN HE SEES THE BLOOD ON THE LINTEL
AND ON THE TWO DOORPOSTS,
THE LORD WILL PASS OVER THE DOOR
AND WILL NOT ALLOW THE DESTROYER
TO COME IN TO YOUR HOUSES TO SMITE YOU.

— EXODUS 12:7, 12–13, 23 —

9

THE BAPTISM OF LOVE

TO DWELL UPON GOD

It is hard for us in this anxious, fearful age to quiet ourselves and meditate in our hearts upon God. We can engage ourselves with Bible study or other acts of obedience. In varying degrees we know how to witness, exhort and bless. We know how to consider these things and even perfect them. But to lift our souls above the material world and consciously dwell upon God Himself seems beyond the reach of our Christian experience.

Yet, to actually grasp the substance of God is to enter the Place of Immunity; it is to receive into our spirits the victory Christ has won. For His sake, we cannot content ourselves merely with good works. Ultimately, we will discover that study and church attendance are but forms that have no satisfaction in and of themselves. These activities must become what the Lord has ordained them to be: *means through which we seek and find God.* Our pleasure will be found not in the mechanics of spiritual disciplines, but that these disciplines bring us closer to the Almighty.

Paul's cry was, **"that I may know Him"** (Phil. 3:10). Paul's desire to know Jesus produced a knowledge of salvation, church order, evangelism and end time events. Out of his heart's passion to know God came revelation, the writing of Scriptures and knowledge of the Eternal.

Paul's knowledge was based upon his *experience* with Christ. Yet, we have satisfied ourselves with a system of historic *facts* about God without pressing into the *reality* of God. The very purpose of the Bible's inspiration is to compel us to find the living God. If the Scriptures have not transferred to us this basic desire for God, our relationship to the Word of the Lord is superficial.

Our goal is to seek earnestly for God until we find Him. Theological knowledge is merely the first step toward the Place of Immunity; it is the map which leads to the country. For too long we have argued concerning the doctrinally correct way to approach God, without truly entering His Presence ourselves. We debate the proper way to interpret the map God has given us without genuinely embarking on the journey.

LOVE WHICH SURPASSES KNOWLEDGE

There is a place greater than knowledge where we abide in Christ's love. This is, indeed, the Place of Immunity. The apostle's prayer for you and me is that we would **"know the love of Christ which surpasses knowledge"** (Eph. 3:19). There is a dwelling place of love that God desires us to enter.

It is a place where our knowledge of God is fulfilled with the substance of God.

We cannot truly know God without, in some way, also experiencing His Person. If you had never seen a sunrise or a starry night sky, could any description substitute for your own eyes beholding their expansive beauty? Likewise, to truly know God we must seek Him until we pass through our knowledge into an encounter with the Almighty.

The "upward call" of God draws us through our doctrines into the certainty, the immediacy, of the Divine Presence. The journey leaves us in the place of surrender, where we yield our being into His hands. We must learn how to listen to Him; as we hear, our call is to then ascend higher to the dwelling place of love.

The last great move of God in the earth shall be distinguished by overwhelming love, *a baptism of love,* poured out from Christ to His people—returned again, with our praise, back to Him. For those who truly yearn for Jesus there shall come, in ever-increasing waves, Christ's deep, fulfilling love.

Yes, His cross shall break us; indeed, His holiness shall purify us. But it shall be His love that floods our being with Himself.

Is this possible, my Lord? Is it true that I might know the love of God which surpasses all knowledge? Oh God, I seek to know You, to live in the substance of Your love. For Your love is the stronghold of my protection.

Help me, Master, to recognize Your love not as a divine emotion but as Your very substance! Help me to see that it was neither Pilate nor Satan that put You on the cross; it was love alone to which You succumbed. Remind me again that it is Your love which still intercedes for me even now.

FLOODED WITH GOD

MAY CHRIST THROUGH YOUR FAITH
[ACTUALLY] DWELL—SETTLE DOWN, ABIDE,
MAKE HIS PERMANENT HOME—IN YOUR HEARTS!

MAY YOU BE ROOTED DEEP IN LOVE
AND FOUNDED SECURELY ON LOVE,
THAT YOU MAY HAVE THE POWER
AND BE STRONG TO APPREHEND
AND GRASP WITH ALL THE SAINTS
(GOD'S DEVOTED PEOPLE,
THE EXPERIENCE OF THAT LOVE)
WHAT IS THE BREADTH AND LENGTH AND HEIGHT
AND DEPTH [OF IT];
[THAT YOU MAY REALLY COME]
TO KNOW—PRACTICALLY,
THROUGH EXPERIENCE FOR YOURSELVES—
THE LOVE OF CHRIST,
WHICH FAR SURPASSES MERE KNOWLEDGE
(WITHOUT EXPERIENCE);
THAT YOU MAY BE FILLED
(THROUGH ALL YOUR BEING)
UNTO ALL THE FULLNESS OF GOD—
[THAT IS] MAY HAVE THE RICHEST MEASURE
OF THE DIVINE PRESENCE, AND BECOME A BODY
WHOLLY FILLED AND FLOODED
WITH GOD HIMSELF

— EPHESIANS 3:17–19 AMPLIFIED —

10

WHERE EVERY
PRAYER IS ANSWERED

We should not assume that simply because we are Christians we have learned the secret of abiding in Christ. Jesus said, **"If you abide in Me, and My words abide in you, ask whatever you wish, and it shall be done for you"** (John 15:7). To abide in Him is to live in ceaseless fusion with His passions. It is to have found the habitation of God where no barrier or shadow exists between our weakness and His sufficiency, or between our yearning and His fulfillment.

Considering the size of God's promises, it is actually a misfortune that most of us have no more than a few minutes of devotions each day and a church service or two a week. The Place of Immunity is not only a place to visit God but to dwell with Him. For those who dwell with God, His Presence is not merely our refuge, it is a permanent address.

When we are abiding in Christ, even as He and the Father are One, so we become one with Him. It is His life, His virtue, His wisdom and His Spirit which sustain us. We become perfectly weak, unable to resist Him. Like the Son's relationship with the Father, so we do nothing from our own initiative unless it is something we see Him do.

If He should require of us nothing more than our love, we are well content. Jesus is our first choice, not our last resort. To those who have entered the abiding place, our questions are not about doctrines or pronouncing the right prayer at an altar. We have found Him whom our soul loves. We are constrained and guided by His voice, surrendered and imprisoned in His love.

He says, **"O my dove, in the clefts of the rock, in the secret place of the steep pathway, let me see your form, let me hear your voice; for your voice is sweet, and your form is lovely"** (Song of Sol. 2:14).

This communion of heart between Christ and His bride is a Place of Immunity. It is God's shelter from the distresses and distractions of life. Here He tells us what to pray; here our supplications are answered. Yet, in spite of our flaws and the weakness of our prayers, to Him our voice is sweet; in spite of our lowliness, our form is lovely in His eyes.

IN THE BOSOM OF CHRIST

What are we to Jesus? Has He given us life only to test His creative skills? No. We exist for the fulfillment of His love. **"As He had loved those who were His own in the world, He loved them to the last and to the highest degree"** (John 13:1 AMPLIFIED).

You are loved by the Lord. He appreciates you. Jesus personally died for each of us; He prays to the Father for us by name. You say, *"But I am full of fears, wrought with failure."* He says, **"Father, they are Your gift to Me"** (John 17:24 NAB).

Christ appreciates us because we are a gift to Him from the Father. Jesus knows that the Father only gives good gifts (James 1:17). Yes, we are imperfect, but Christ sees us in our ultimate completeness. Seeing the end from the beginning, He joyfully receives us.

And what kind of gift are we? Are we a reward or, perhaps, a challenge? No. We are His bride. The glance of our eyes makes His heart beat faster (Song of Sol. 4:9). And it is here, in the love we share with Jesus, that we are secured in the Place of Immunity.

Lord, forgive me for the inconsistency of my commitment to You. Lord, I abandon any dwelling place of self. Grant me Your power that I might truly abide in You; grant me obedience that I might sustain Your abiding Word in me. With all that I am, I desire unbroken fellowship with You. Even now, shape me to fit perfectly into Your Presence, that I might dwell in oneness with You, that I might live empowered by the impulse of Your will.

BECAUSE WE LOVE HIM

"BECAUSE HE HAS LOVED ME,
THEREFORE I WILL DELIVER HIM;
I WILL SET HIM SECURELY ON HIGH,
BECAUSE HE HAS KNOWN MY NAME.

"HE WILL CALL UPON ME,
AND I WILL ANSWER HIM;
I WILL BE WITH HIM IN TROUBLE;
I WILL RESCUE HIM, AND HONOR HIM.
WITH A LONG LIFE I WILL SATISFY HIM,
AND LET HIM BEHOLD MY SALVATION."

— PSALM 91:14–16 —

11

THE POWER
OF HIS NAME

ONENESS WITH CHRIST

**"And whatever you ask in My name, that will I do,
that the Father may be glorified in the Son"** (John 14:13).
With what earnestness we have read Christ's words:
"Whatever you ask . . . I will do." How is it that this promise
is not fulfilled for us? Why is it that such great anticipation
results in such a small return?

Think of the implications if Jesus' words are actually
true! Any sickness can be healed; any demon can be cast out.
Any sinner, friend or relative can be saved. He said, **"Whatever you ask."** Who is to stop our faith from reaching even
a greater fulfillment? Not only can any person be healed, but

also any city; not merely can any demon be cast out, but any principality can be brought down. The ends of the earth await the awakening of our faith to Christ's promise!

Yet, like the rich young ruler, we know something is missing in us. We ask the Master, *"What still do we lack?"* In the gospel of John, Jesus continues, **"If you ask Me anything in My name, I will do it. If you love Me, you will keep My commandments"** (John 14:14–15). *Jesus will not spontaneously answer our requests until we instinctively obey His.* Obedience to His requests prepares us to experience His indwelling, where His love finds its fulfillment.

It is vital that we obey Him, but Christ's ultimate goal is not only our obedience: it is our oneness with Him. He would rather dwell intimately in just one of His servants' hearts than to have ten thousand who know Him from afar. He is after our love. And what is love? It is a passion for oneness.

"He who has My commandments and keeps them, he it is who loves Me; and he who loves Me shall be loved by My Father, and I will love him, and will disclose Myself to him" (John 14:21). Obedience born of love leads to greater love; greater love ultimately leads to the open disclosure of Christ to our hearts.

"I will love him, and will disclose Myself to him." Let us read these words over and over again. Let us arouse our spirits to the deep, holy desire that not only dwells in Christ's promise, but also in His heart. Jesus longed for continued fellowship with His disciples. Thus, He was preparing them for intimacy with Himself *after* His resurrection.

IN HIS NAME

"Intimacy with Jesus." "Oneness with Jesus." What do these words mean except that the union of Christ and His church has engendered a new creation, a new species of man that is part earth-born, part heaven-born. As such, we have access into the Presence of God; from here we stand as intercessors for the needs of man. Yet, we also come as God's ambassadors, bringing His word to man and entreating them, on behalf of Christ, to be reconciled to God.

So, Jesus promises: **"Whatever you ask of the Father in My name"** He will provide (John 15:16). The key to unlocking His promise is the phrase, **"in My name."** The fact is, all of God's promises are accessed through the name of Jesus.

Jesus' name is His divine and kingly seal, His signature on our marching orders. As we are one with Him in intimacy, so we become one with Him in purpose. He said, **"As the Father has sent Me, I also send you"** (John 20:21). Thus, our prayer is more truly Christ's prayer expressed through us to the Father. As those whom Christ has commissioned and sent forth in the redemptive purpose, we approach God as Christ's earthly representatives. His "name" is synonymous with His mission, which is to see the lost of this world saved; the wounded, healed; and the demonized, delivered.

Once, I asked a new secretary to call a certain church leader who is a good friend of mine. She called, but because the individual was very busy, she was unable to get through. After reporting back to me that she could not reach him, I asked her if she had mentioned to my friend's secretary that she was calling for Francis Frangipane. She had not. So, I told her to call again using my name. This time she was immediately put through, for he was expecting my call. She gained access not on the basis of *her* relationship with him but through *my* relationship with him. What she presented to him was not *her* needs and requests but *mine*. The information my secretary sought was granted because she came in my name representing my purpose.

Likewise, we come to God through Jesus' perfect relationship with Him. On the highest level, we come representing Christ, not ourselves. To the degree we come to God with Jesus' thoughts and motives, we receive power to fulfill Jesus' purpose.

Using the name of Jesus in prayer does not mean I can ask for and receive anything I desire, except where my desires are conformed to the desires of Christ. In other words, I cannot simply attach a religious postscript, "In Jesus' name," at the end of a selfish prayer and expect to always be answered. No. Not until our hearts become purely motivated with Christ's purposes will our prayers return empowered with heaven's resources.

What about our personal needs? Our greatest personal need is to know Jesus. It is here, in our intimacy with Christ and His word, that all we need for ourselves is supplied. Did not Jesus say that if we sought first for God's kingdom, all we would ever need on earth would be added unto us (Matt. 6:33)? You see, our confidence in prayer comes from Christ's relationship with the Father; while our joy in life comes from our relationship with Christ.

The more we truly come to know Jesus by abiding in Him and His word abiding in us, we represent Him as we approach the Father in His name. It is here that He assures us, **"Ask whatever you wish, and it shall be done for you"** (John 15:7).

AGAINST THE ENEMY

The expression *in His name* also speaks of the authority Christ has given us in spiritual warfare. We not only represent Christ's interests to the Father, we use the authority in

His name against the devil—and whatever else resists God's revealed purpose. In His name every knee shall bow and every tongue confess His Lordship.

We are Christ's ambassadors. In the world, those who serve as ambassadors are chosen because of their mastery at representing the interests of their ruler. They have been proven trustworthy; they know the *heart* of their leader. The most skilled ambassador is one who best represents his lord's intent. Because the emissary continually draws upon his leader's instructions, the word of the ambassador becomes as binding as the word of the king himself.

So, our oneness with Christ prepares us to mirror His will and to represent His purpose. Whether we are approaching God's throne in Christ's redemptive purpose or assaulting the strongholds of hell in Christ's eternal judgment, we come in the name of Jesus Christ! This is why we can ask whatever we will and it shall be granted: *We come in the authority of Jesus Christ!* Abiding in Jesus' name is our Place of Immunity.

What name is like Thy name, Lord Jesus? When I speak Your name in worship, it is like honey on my lips; when I utter it in battle it is a weapon no enemy can oppose. Give me grace, Master, to fully represent You in every aspect of life, to go forth from this moment in the power of Your name!

Ask Me Anything

And whatever you ask
in My name,
that will I do,
that the Father
may be glorified
in the Son.

If you ask Me anything
in My name,
I will do it.

—John 14:13–14—

12

"THIS TIME I WILL PRAISE THE LORD"

DISAPPOINTMENTS ARE INEVITABLE

We cannot pass through life without getting hurt. Pain and disappointment in this world are inevitable. But how we handle our setbacks shapes our character and prepares us for eternity. Our attitudes are the pivotal factor determining the level of our immunity from strife.

Regardless of the hardships we have faced and in spite of the mistakes we have made, the end of our lives can either be full of praise and thanksgiving or misery and complaint. In the final analysis, what we have experienced in life will be as rich as the desires we have had fulfilled or as painful as the things we regret.

The Bible tells us, **"Hope deferred makes the heart sick"** (Prov. 13:12). Those deep disappointments in life have a way of never leaving us; they enter our hearts like fire and then harden into our nature like lava. Setbacks can leave us cautious about new ventures and suspicious of new friends. Our woundedness restricts our openness. We are fearful we will be hurt again by new relationships.

Gradually, unless we learn to handle heartache correctly, we become embittered and resentful cynics. We lose the joy of being alive.

THE SOURCE OF FULFILLMENT

It is our own desires and the degree of their fulfillment that produce either joy or sorrow in our lives. Even basic desires for marriage or friends can enslave us if they consume our attention. Are these desires evil? No, but if having our desires fulfilled is the main reason we have come to Christ, it is possible our lives simply will not improve until our priorities change.

The Lord *is* concerned about fulfilling our desires, but to do so He must pry our fingers off our lives and turn our hearts toward Him. Indeed, the reason we are alive is not to fulfill our desires but to become His worshipers.

Personal fulfillment can become an idol; it can develop into such an obsession that we are living for happiness more than living for God. Thus, part of our salvation includes having our desires prioritized by Christ. In the Sermon on the Mount, He put it this way: **"But seek first His kingdom and His righteousness; and all these things shall be added to you. Therefore do not be anxious for tomorrow; for tomorrow will care for itself"** (Matt. 6:33–34). God wants to, and will, satisfy us beyond our dreams but not before He is first in our hearts.

A wonderful example of this can be seen in the life of Leah, Jacob's first wife. Leah was unattractive, unwanted and unloved by her husband. Jacob had served Laban, Leah's father, seven years for Rachel, who was Leah's younger sister. On their wedding night, however, Laban put Leah in the nuptial tent instead of Rachel. Although Jacob actually did marry Rachel a week later, he had to work another seven years for her. So Jacob had two wives who were sisters. And the Scriptures tell us that Rachel was loved by Jacob but Leah was "hated" (lit. Hebrews).

"Now the Lord saw that Leah was unloved" (Gen. 29:31). We must understand this about the nature of God: *The Lord is drawn to those who hurt.* **"The Lord saw . . . Leah."** What wonderful words! In the same way water descends and fills that which is lowest, so Christ reaches first to the afflicted to fill the lowliest and comfort them.

The Lord saw that Leah was unloved. He saw her pain, loneliness and heartache. Leah, though unloved by Jacob, was deeply loved by the Lord and He gave her a son. Leah's reaction was predictable. She said, **"Surely now my husband will love me"** (v. 32).

Worse than living your life alone is to be married to someone who hates you, as was Leah. How Leah wished that Jacob might share the love he had for Rachel with her. Who could blame her? Leah's desires were justified. She had given him a first-born son. In her mind, if the Lord could open her womb, He could also open Jacob's heart. But the time was not yet; Jacob still did not love her.

Twice more Leah gave birth to sons and each time her desire was for her husband. She said, **"Now this time my husband will become attached to me, because I have borne him three sons"** (v. 34). Yet, Jacob's heart did not desire her.

For Leah, as well as for us, there is a lesson here: *You cannot make another person love you.* In fact, the more pressure you place upon others to accept you, the more likely they are to reject you instead. Leah's concept of fulfillment was based on attaining Jacob's love and now her problem was worsening. For not only was she unattractive to Jacob but her jealousies were adding to her lack of loveliness.

Three times we read in this text that the Lord saw and heard that Leah was unloved. He had seen her affliction. Through all her striving for Jacob and her disappointment with her marital relationship, the Lord was tenderly wooing Leah to Himself.

As Leah became pregnant a fourth time, a miracle of grace occurred within her. She gradually became aware that, while she had not been the focus of her husband's love, she was loved by God. And as this fourth pregnancy drew near to completion, she drew nearer and nearer to God. She became a worshiper of the Almighty.

Now as she gave birth to another son, she said, **"This time I will praise the Lord"** (v. 35). She named that child *Judah,* which means "praise." It was from the tribe of Judah that Christ was born.

Leah had been seeking self-fulfillment and found only heartache and pain. But as she became a worshiper of God, she entered life's highest fulfillment: *She began to please God.*

It is right here that the human soul truly begins to change and enter the Place of Immunity. As she found fulfillment in God, He began to remove from her the jealousies, insecurities and heartaches that life had conveyed to her. A true inner beauty started growing in Leah; she became a woman at rest.

Likewise, we each have character defects that we are reluctant or unable to face. Others have seen these things in us but they have lacked the courage to tell us. Both physically and personally, these flaws in our nature are what leave us anxious, threatened and unfulfilled.

It is not counsel or classes on success or self-esteem that we need; we simply need to discover God's love for us. As we begin to praise Him in all things, we simultaneously put on the garments of salvation. We are actually being *saved* from that which would otherwise have destroyed us! Disappointments and heartaches cannot cling to us, for we are worshipers of God! And, **"God causes all things to work together for good to those who *love* God"** (Rom. 8:28). If we continue to love God, nothing we experience can ultimately turn out harmful!

THE TREE OF LIFE

You will remember the verse we quoted, **"Hope deferred makes the heart sick"** (Prov. 13:12). But the verse concludes with, **"but desire fulfilled is a tree of life."** *As our desires are fulfilled, we are fulfilled.* Since it is the fulfillment of our desires which fills us with satisfaction, the secret to a rewarding life is to commit our desires to God. Let Him choose the times and means of our fulfillment, allowing the Lord to prepare us for Himself along the way. The truth is that in ourselves we are incomplete; but in Christ we have been made complete (Col. 2:10).

You say, *"That's easy for you to say. You have a wonderful wife and family. You are blessed. But you don't understand my problems."* Yes, I do. My wonderful marriage was very difficult for the first few years. We struggled with many things in our relationship. My wife and I both came to the place where we were unfulfilled in each other. But, like Leah, we both looked to God and said, **"This time I will praise the Lord."** In fact, we named our second child the very name Leah gave to her fourth—*Judah.*

For us, as for Leah, our lives were turned around as we chose to delight in God *in spite of being unfulfilled with each other.* As we became His worshipers, He began to work on our hearts until we were not only more pleasing to Him, we were also pleasing to each other! What I am relating to you is the very thing that saved and blessed our marriage!

Psalms 37:4 reads, **"Delight yourself in the Lord; and He will give you the desires of your heart."** As you delight in God, you change. The negative effects of disappointment and grief fall off. As love and joy from God begin to fulfill us, our very souls are restored and beautified. Yes, delight yourself with Jesus and your self-destructive tendencies will actually begin to vanish. Christ will beautify your life from the inside out.

THE OUTCOME OF LEAH'S LIFE

What happened with Leah? Well, the long years came and went. In time, Rachel and then Leah died. Jacob, on his deathbed, spoke to his sons: **"I am about to be gathered to my people; bury me with my fathers in the cave . . . which Abraham bought . . . for a burial site. There they buried Abraham and his wife Sarah, there they buried Isaac and his wife Rebekah, and there I buried Leah—"** (Gen. 49:29–31).

Jacob had buried *Leah* in the ancestral place of honor! Oh how those words, though few, say so much! They tell us that God had beautified this afflicted one with salvation. After Leah found fulfillment in God, He gave her fulfillment in Jacob. Over the years, inner peace and spiritual beauty shone forth from Leah; Jacob was knit to her in love. It is not hard to imagine that when Leah died, she left smiling, with the praises of God upon her lips.

Become a worshiper of God! As you surrender your desires to Him, as you put Him first, He will take what you give Him and make it beautiful in its time. He will take what has been bent and imbalanced within you and make you stand upright in His light and glory.

Therefore, this day speak to your soul. Tell the areas of unfulfillment within you that *this time you will praise the Lord!*

Lord, I am a Leah, unlovely and always seeking the love of those who have rejected me. How foolish I have been. How blind. There is no love, no fulfillment in this life apart from You. You are the Tree of Life that satisfies all desires; You are the Healer of my heart. I love You, Lord Jesus.

A Stronghold
for the Oppressed

The Lord also will be
a stronghold for the oppressed,
A stronghold
in times of trouble,

And those who know
Thy name
will put their trust in Thee;
For Thou, O Lord,
hast not forsaken
those who seek Thee.

— Psalm 9:9–10 —

13

A THANKFUL HEART

The very quality of your life, whether you love it or hate it, is based upon how thankful you are toward God. Our attitude determines whether life is to us a place of blessedness or wretchedness and misery. Indeed, looking at the same rose bush, some people complain that the roses have thorns while others rejoice that roses come with the thorns! It all depends on your perspective.

This is the only life you will have before you enter eternity. If you want to find joy, you must first find thankfulness. Indeed, the one who is thankful for even a little enjoys much. But the unappreciative soul is always miserable, always complaining. He lives outside the Place of Immunity.

Perhaps the worst enemy we have is not the devil but our own tongue. James tells us, **"the tongue is set among our members as that which ... sets on fire the course of our** life" (James 3:6). He goes on to say this fire is ignited by hell. Consider: With our own words we can enter the spirit of heaven or the agonies of hell!

It is hell, with its punishments, torments and misery, which controls the life of the grumbler and complainer! Paul expands this thought in 1 Corinthians 10:10, where he reminds us of the Jews who **"grumble[d] and were destroyed by the destroyer."** The fact is, every time we open up to grumbling and complaining, the quality of our life is reduced proportionally—a *destroyer* is bringing our life to ruin!

People often ask me, "What is the ruling demon over our church or city?" They expect me to answer with the ancient Aramaic or Phoenician name of a fallen angel. What I usually tell them is a lot more practical: One of the most pervasive evil influences over our nation is *ingratitude!*

Do not minimize the strength and cunning of this enemy! Paul said that the Jews who grumbled and complained during their difficult circumstances were **"destroyed by the destroyer."** Who was this *destroyer?* If you insist on discerning an ancient world ruler, one of the most powerful spirits mentioned in the Bible is Abaddon, whose Greek name is *Apollyon.* It means "destroyer" (Rev. 9:11). Paul said the Jews were destroyed by this spirit. In other words, *when we are complaining or unthankful, we open the door to the destroyer, Abaddon, the demon-king over the abyss of hell!*

IN THE PRESENCE OF GOD

Multitudes in our nation have become specialists in the "science of misery." They are experts—moral accountants—who can, in a moment, tally all the wrongs society has ever done to them or their group. I have never talked with one of these people who was happy, blessed or content about anything. They expect an imperfect world to treat them perfectly.

Truly, there *are* people in this wounded country of ours who need special attention. However, most of us simply need to repent of ingratitude, for it is ingratitude itself which is keeping wounds alive! We simply need to forgive the wrongs of the past and become thankful for what we have in the present.

The moment we become grateful, we actually begin to ascend spiritually into the Presence of God. The psalmist wrote,

> **Serve the Lord with gladness; come before Him with joyful singing. Enter His gates with thanksgiving, and His courts with praise. Give thanks to Him; bless His name. For the Lord is good; His lovingkindness is everlasting, and His faithfulness to all generations.** —Psalm 100:2, 4–5

It does not matter what your circumstances are, the instant you begin to thank God, even though your situation has not changed, *you* begin to change. The key which unlocks the gates of heaven is a thankful heart; entrance into the courts of God comes as you simply begin to praise the Lord.

A THANKFUL MAN IS A HUMBLE MAN

If you think you know God but do not live your life in gratitude before Him, it is doubtful that you really knew Him in the first place. A thankful heart honors God. Often when we say we "know God," what we really mean is that we know facts *about* God. But we should ask ourselves, *"Do I truly know Him?"*

Paul warns that just knowing doctrines about God is not enough to enter eternal life. He said,

For since the creation of the world His invisible attributes, His eternal power and divine nature, have been clearly seen, being understood through what has been made, so that they are without excuse.

For even though they knew God, they did not honor Him as God, or give thanks; but they became futile in their speculations, and their foolish heart was darkened. —Romans 1:20–21

Even though we may know God, if we do not honor Him *as* God and thank Him for ruling in our lives, our thoughts turn foolish and our minds darken. When we are in that ungrateful state of mind, every word we speak is a spark lit by hell, set to feed upon and consume our joy and hope in this world.

H.W. Beecher said, *"Pride slays thanksgiving... a proud man is seldom a grateful man, for he never thinks he gets as much as he deserves."* We should be thankful that we do *not* get what we deserve, for each of us deserves hell! When adversities or the small irritations of life come your way, be thankful you are not getting what you deserve!

The truth is, God's plan allows for problems so He can teach us to, **"Rejoice always; pray without ceasing; in everything give thanks."** The Bible tells us that these attitudes are **"God's will for you in Christ Jesus"** (1 Thess. 5:16–18). Are small irritations God's will? No. *Rejoicing* in the difficulty is God's will; that you remain *thankful* during the crisis is God's will.

It is obvious that the Lord does not want us to succumb to defeat, for it is His will that we **"pray without ceasing."**

He did not say "accept the difficulties." He said to pray, continue to rejoice and remain vocally thankful. As you do, your circumstances will be established in victory!

This very thing happened to me during a time of great difficulty in the beginning of my ministry. I was battling with poverty, disappointment and the struggle of guiding our congregation's growth. I knew I was at a crossroads. But, as long as I thought I deserved more, I was not thankful for what the Lord had given me.

When God gives us less than we desire, it is not because He is teaching us poverty; He is teaching us thankfulness. *You see, life—real life—is not based upon what we amass, but on what we enjoy.* In those very circumstances God had given me much to appreciate, but I could not see it because my heart was wrong. Once I repented and simply began to enjoy the church He had given me, my whole life changed.

God wants us to be blessed, to prosper with the real things of life. However, if we are distracted by comparing ourselves to other churches or other people, how can we appreciate what He has given us? We simply need to be grateful.

Someone once said, *"When I see a poor man who is grateful, I know if he were rich, he would be generous."* A thankful spirit is akin to a generous spirit, for both appreciate and receive the riches of God. When we are thankful with little, God can entrust us with much.

OUT OF ZION GOD HAS SHOWN FORTH

"The Mighty One, God, the Lord, has spoken, and summoned the earth from the rising of the sun to its setting. Out of Zion, the perfection of beauty, God has shone forth" (Ps. 50:1–2). God shines forth out of Zion. It is this God, who beautifies His creation with His Presence, that calls His people into covenant union. To accomplish the glorification of His people, the Lord calls, **"Gather My godly ones to Me, those who have made a covenant with Me by sacrifice"** (Ps. 50:5).

To make a covenant with someone is to enjoin ourselves in the most solemn bonds of unity. As we said earlier, a covenant is more than a promise; it is the pledge of two lives to live as one. The union God seeks with us is called a *covenant of sacrifice.*

This covenant is not a ritual form of worship; it is not the Jewish sacrifice of bulls and goats. It transcends time and methodology and reaches to every soul who longs for the living God. It is a covenant of thanksgiving. He says,

> **Gather My godly ones to Me, those who have made a covenant with Me by sacrifice. I know every bird of the mountains, and everything that moves in the field is Mine.**
>
> **Offer to God a sacrifice of thanksgiving, and pay your vows to the Most High; He who offers a sacrifice of thanksgiving honors Me; And to him who orders his way aright I shall show the salvation of God.** —Psalm 50:5, 11, 14, 23

The terms of the covenant are simple: We pledge to thank Him and adore Him in everything; He pledges to shine forth from our lives in the perfection of beauty. It is a *sacrifice* of thanksgiving, for it will cost us to praise Him when we hurt. But to do so is part of our healing and the beginning of our salvation.

Begin to thank Him. Name the gifts He has given you, starting with the blessing of life itself. When we thank Him, we are honoring Him.

Today God is calling for His people to enter into a covenant bond with Him—a covenant where we pledge to live a thankful life and He pledges His life to shine forth through us. This covenant of thanksgiving is the key which shuts and bolts the door to demonic oppression in a person's life. It is a glorious gate into the Place of Immunity.

Blessed Lord, forgive me for being a complainer. Help me to offer to You the sacrifice of thanksgiving in all things. Lord, I come this day to covenant with You. By Your grace, I will be thankful regardless of what my life seems to be. Oh God, remember Your covenant pledge and gather me near to Your heart. In Jesus' name. Amen.

A Strong Tower!

The name of the Lord
is a strong tower;
The righteous
runs into it
and is safe.

— Proverbs 18:10 —

14

THE VALLEY
OF FRUITFULNESS

The battles we face are often intense times of weakness, distress and confusion. If the events of our lives were charted, these would be the lowest points. Yet, God is no less with us during difficulties than at other times. In fact, these valleys are often as much the plan of God as our mountaintop experiences.

There is a story in the Bible which speaks plainly to this truth. Israel had recently defeated the Arameans in a mountain battle. In 1 Kings, chapter 20, we read,

Then the prophet came near to the king of Israel, and said to him, "Go, strengthen yourself and observe and see what you have to do; for at the

> turn of the year the king of Aram will come up against you." Now the servants of the king of Aram said to him, "Their gods are gods of the mountains, therefore they were stronger than we; but rather let us fight against them in the plain, and surely we shall be stronger than they."
>
> —1 Kings 20:22–23

The enemy said that the God of Israel was a god of the mountains, but if they fought the Jews in the valleys they would defeat them. We read in verse 28,

> Then a man of God came near and spoke to the king of Israel and said, "Thus says the Lord, 'Because the Arameans have said, "The Lord is a god of the mountains, but He is not a god of the valleys"; therefore, I will give all this great multitude into your hand, and you shall know that I am the Lord.' "
>
> —1 Kings 20:28

No matter what the enemy tries to tell you, Christ is God of the mountains *and* God of the valleys. He has not stopped being God because you happen to be in a valley. He is the God of glory, as seen in His power and miracles. In the valleys, He reveals Himself as faithful, loyally committed to us in difficulties and distresses. In and through all things, He is our God.

When we are on the "mountaintops" of our Christian experience, we can see our future clearly. We have perspective and confidence. However, when we are in one of life's valleys, our vision is limited and our future seems hidden. Yet, valleys are also the most fertile places on earth. *Valleys produce fruitfulness.* You can expect there to be a harvest of virtue when God dwells with you in the valleys.

THE HIGHWAY TO ZION

"How blessed is the man whose strength is in Thee; in whose heart are the highways to Zion! Passing through the valley of Baca, they make it a spring" (Ps. 84:5–6). *Baca* means "weeping." Each of us has times of weeping when our hearts and hopes seem crushed. However, because God has placed in our hearts "highways to Zion," we *pass through* valleys; we do not live in them.

"Passing through the valley of Baca . . ." Once we are on the other side of weeping, our Redeemer makes it "a spring." The very things which overwhelmed us will, in time, refresh us with new life. Whether we are experiencing the height of success and power or are in a valley of weakness and despair, the Lord is our God continually!

Has the enemy isolated you, causing you to doubt God's love? Do not forget, while we were yet sinners, Christ died for us. Even the hairs on your head are numbered. He cares. It is His love for us that redeems our hardships, which not only brings good out of what was meant for evil but also trains us to deliver others.

How did Jesus prepare to do wonderful works? Part of His training involved suffering. Christ was a man of sorrows; He was One who was acquainted with grief. Yet, His suffering was the Father's means of acquainting Him with the actual feelings of mankind's need and pain. Because He suffered what we suffer, He is able to serve as a faithful high priest. If we yield to God's plan for Christ to be formed in us, God will take our sorrows to enlarge our hearts. Once we have been acquainted with grief, we then can be anointed with compassion to deliver others.

Consider Joseph. He was the second youngest of Jacob's sons and his father's favorite. His walk with God began with dreams and visions. Joseph's life is a pattern for many who have had a genuine call from God. Our walk with God may also have begun with a "travel brochure" of dreams and visions: God gives us a picture of His destination for us. What we do not see is *how* His promises will come to pass in our lives.

Joseph was betrayed by his brothers and delivered up by them to die. He was unjustly accused when Potiphar's wife tried to seduce him. He was imprisoned and forgotten by all except God, who patiently watched and measured Joseph's reaction to difficulty.

Rich or poor, blessed or smitten, Joseph served God. He was being tested, but he continued to pass his tests. Joseph was on trial before men, but he was found innocent before God.

Finally, at the right moment, the Lord suddenly connected all the loose ends of Joseph's life. Everything that Joseph went through would have seemed cruel and unfair, except that the Lord was shaping a man for His purpose. God uses *everything* we go through for future purposes that He alone sees. We do not see His ultimate plan while we are in the valley; we must *remember* the vision, keeping faith in what God has promised.

Just as He allowed Joseph to go through many trials, so He allows us to go through great conflicts as well. For He knows that our lives—what we have become through His grace—will help others find the Place of Immunity in their lives.

"And Joseph named the first-born Manasseh, 'For,' he said, 'God has made me forget all my trouble and all my father's household' " (Gen. 41:51). God caused Joseph to forget the difficulty and pain of his life. There is something wonderful about the Lord's capacity to cause all things to work for good. With Jesus in our lives, a time ultimately comes when God causes us to forget all the troubles of the past.

"And he named the second Ephraim, 'For,' he said, 'God has made me fruitful in the land of my affliction' " (Gen. 41:52). God made him fruitful in the very things that afflicted him. In the land of your affliction, in your battle, is the place where God will make you fruitful. Consider, even now, the area of greatest affliction in your life. In *that* area God will make you fruit-ful in such a way that your heart will be fully satisfied and God's heart fully glorified.

Ultimately, the Lord will touch many others with the substance of what you have gained. In a world that is superficial, Christ will produce something in you that is deep and living.

> FULFILLING HIS EXTERNAL PLAN IS SECONDARY TO WHAT WE BECOME TO GOD IN THE PROCESS. THE SOONER WE ATTAIN VIRTUE THAT REMAINS CONSISTENT DURING TESTING, THE SOONER WE ATTAIN GOD'S OTHER PROMISES.

God has not promised to keep us from valleys and sufferings but to make us fruitful in them. Without doubt, we each will pass through valleys before we reach our final goal in God. As we remain faithful to Him in trials, the character and nature of Christ Jesus shall emerge in our spirits; Christ shall be revealed to those around us. He intends to make your life a key that unlocks the Place of Immunity for others.

Lord, You are God of the mountains and the valleys. I know that Your faithfulness is my shield and my bulwark. Thank You for redeeming the conflicts of my life; I praise You for healing me and causing me to forget all the trauma of my past.

Now, Lord, help me to not forget what I have learned here. Cause me to remember that the crises in my life always precede the enrichment of my life. Help me to recognize that the place of my fruitfulness is in the land of my affliction. In Jesus' name. Amen.

No Weapon Formed
Against You Shall Prosper

"In righteousness you will be established;
You will be far from oppression,
for you will not fear; and from terror,
for it will not come near you.

If anyone fiercely assails you
it will not be from Me.
Whoever assails you
will fall because of you.
Behold, I Myself have created the smith
who blows the fire of coals,
And brings out a weapon for its work;
And I have created the destroyer to ruin.

No weapon that is formed against you
shall prosper;
And every tongue that accuses you
in judgment you will condemn.
This is the heritage
of the servants of the Lord,
And their vindication is from Me,"
declares the Lord.

— Isaiah 54:14–17 —

15

A FORGIVING HEART

During the last hours of this age, there will be two opposing factions in the world: those whose hearts are wrought with bitterness, resentment and hatred, and those whose love has actually increased and are experiencing the power of the kingdom of God. Jesus foretold these conditions in Matthew. He said, **"many will fall away and will deliver up one another and hate one another . . . and because lawlessness (iniquity) is increased, most people's love will grow cold"** (Matt. 24:10–12). But then He added, **"This gospel of the kingdom shall be preached in the whole world for a witness to all the nations, and then the end shall come"** (Matt. 24:14).

What is this "gospel of the kingdom"? It is the whole truth Jesus came to bring, not only that which saves us from our sins but that which creates us in His image. It is the full gospel with all its requirements and all its rewards: the full price for the full power. It is the most glorious pearl that man can possess: the Presence of God in glory revealed within and among us.

Thus, if we are to attain this great love, we will continually be forced to make the choice between mercy and unforgiveness. If we do not walk in a forgiving attitude, we will certainly become prey to an embittered spirit. If it is, indeed, God's plan to allow wickedness and holiness to simultaneously grow to full maturity, then we must guard our hearts beforehand from reacting in bitterness and unforgiveness. The increasing lawlessness will certainly give us occasions to lose love.

Yet, just to survive in this cruel world, we often withdraw from the vulnerability of love. We cannot choose cautious, selective love and also walk in the power of God's kingdom. To counter pain, we unconsciously shut down our love, for it is love that makes us vulnerable. God wants us to be a people whose love is growing hot, not cold.

Jesus did not say we had to *trust* our enemies, but He did say we had to *love* them. You ask, "Why?" One reason God allows difficulties is to test us. He wants to see if our Christianity is merely an intellectual pursuit or if following Him is truly the highest passion of our hearts. Thus, He tells us, **"love your enemies, and pray for those who persecute you"** (Matt. 5:44).

Some of you have gone through rejection and betrayal, but the Lord says you did not fail. You have continued to love. Although you went through great pain, you have forgiven those who have hurt you. You passed the test.

Some of us still have certain individuals in our lives that we have not forgiven and whom we do not love. Perhaps you are right, they do not deserve your forgiveness. But, what you do not realize is the consequence of your anger.

As long as you refuse to forgive, a part of you is trapped in the past where you are continually being reminded of your pain. Even the calendar season in which you were hurt stimulates depression and foreboding! Until you forgive, you will not be fully released to go on with your life.

There is only one way we can have true fellowship with God and that is in the "here and now." But when your mind is harboring unforgiveness, you are neither in the "here" nor in the "now." When you live in the past, you are cut off from God. What they did to you is over. It is done. It does not have any real existence or life of its own *except in your mind.*

There, within you, the conflict continues to live—and as long as it lives, you are still being hurt by it. The person who wounded you may have long since died. They cannot be blamed, for it is *you* who keeps your wounds alive!

Not only is the quality of your spiritual life affected, but your physical well-being pays a price as well. As long as you keep holding onto the burden of what someone did to you, each time you think about that person your stomach acids churn and your anxiety increases. Your body is continually put under stress.

If you do not forgive those who have hurt you, you will lose a measure of your capacity to love. Whether they deserve forgiveness or not, *you* deserve a better life! And God wants to give you a better life. But you cannot enjoy abundant life while carrying unforgiveness, for you are shackled to something that hurt you, and your own unforgiveness tortures you.

How do you get out of that prison? How do you find the protection of God for your soul? God calls you to forgive. You must see the hands of God reaching to you in the midst of your pain. He wants to redeem that conflict, using that specific adversity to perfect character in you. It will be this event that He will use to make you like Christ, and to become like Christ is to abide in the Place of Immunity.

Each time you say, *"Father, I choose to love, I choose to forgive, I choose to forget and not hold it against that person,"* you are taking on Christ's nature. Rejoice! Jesus is taking over your heart! You are entering the Place of Immunity.

Master, I see in Your forgiveness of me the pattern for my forgiveness of others. Lord, You forgave the Pharisees who lied about You; You pardoned the soldiers who mocked and crucified You; You encouraged Your disciples' hearts to not be troubled, knowing they were about to deny and betray You.

Yet, You not only forgave them, You died for them. You opened Your heart as wide as the universe and welcomed us all to be reconciled to God. Grant me this power to forgive, to lay down my life for others, to know the love that compelled You to such righteousness! Amen.

As He Is,
So Also Are We

Beloved, let us love one another,
for love is from God; and everyone who
loves is born of God and knows God.
The one who does not love
does not know God,
for God is love.

And we have come to know and have
believed the love which God has for us.
God is love,
and the one who abides in love
abides in God, and God abides in him.

By this, love is perfected with us,
that we may have confidence
in the day of judgment; because as He is,
so also are we in this world.

— 1 John 4:7–8, 16–17 —

16

LOVE: GOD'S PRESERVATIVE

There will be a time when each of us will stand before Jesus Christ and He will open a door called "reality-past." There, we shall gaze into the days of our earthly existence.

Jesus will not only commend our lives in a general way, but He will point to specific things we did. Rejoicing together with us, He will say, **"Well done!"** Perhaps there was a special act of kindness that turned a bitter person back toward God; or you overcame your fears and led a person to Christ whom God then used to win thousands.

In the Latin translation of the Bible, the phrase *well done* is rendered "Bravo!" How would you like Jesus to say that to you? Imagine Him with His arm around your shoulder, saying, *"Bravo! You were just an average person, but you trusted Me, you learned to love without fear, and look how many hearts we touched together!"* To be so pleasing to Christ that He rejoices over the life we give Him should be our highest goal.

LOVE IN THE MIDST OF PRESSURE

Yet it is here, in a world filled with devils, devil-possessed people and conflicts of all sorts, that we must find the life of Christ. In fact, Jesus warned about the Great Tribulation; one meaning of the word *tribulation* is "pressure." Even today, is not stress and pressure increasing upon people? In spite of these tensions, God has called us to love *extravagantly*. If we do not counteract the stress of this age with love, we will crumble beneath the weight of offenses.

Have you ever seen in a supermarket a shopping cart full of bent food cans? Most have lost their labels. You can buy a half dozen for a dollar or two. What happened is that the atmospheric pressure outside the can was greater then the pressure inside, and the can collapsed. It could not withstand the pressure.

Similarly, we must have an aggressive force pushing out from inside us that is equal to the pressures trying to crumble us from the outside. We need the pressure of God's love pouring out through us, neutralizing the pressures of hatred and bitterness in the world.

Love is God's preservative. It surrounds our souls with a power greater than the power of the devil and the world around us. It keeps us balanced; it insulates us against the hostility that exists in our world. Love is the shelter of the Most High; it is the substance of the Place of Immunity.

Lord, forgive me for looking for some other means of protection besides Your love. Truly, pressures have increased upon my life; stress multiplies daily in our world. Yet, Lord, grant me the eternal equalizer: love. Grant that I would walk in such surrender to You that the power of Your love would unceasingly emanate from my soul. Amen.

Evil Will Not Touch You

Behold, how happy is the man whom God reproves,
So do not despise the discipline of the Almighty.
For He inflicts pain, and gives relief;
He wounds, and His hands also heal.
From six troubles He will deliver you,
Even in seven evil will not touch you.

In famine He will redeem you from death,
And in war from the power of the sword.
You will be hidden from the scourge of the tongue,
Neither will you be afraid of violence
when it comes.
You will laugh at violence and famine,
Neither will you be afraid of wild beasts.

For you will be in league with the stones
of the field; And the beasts of the field
will be at peace with you.
And you will know that your tent is secure,
For you will visit your abode and fear no loss.
You will know also that your descendants
will be many, And your offspring
as the grass of the earth.
You will come to the grave in full vigor,
Like the stacking of grain in its season.
Behold this, we have investigated it,
Thus it is; Hear it, and know for yourself.

— Job 5:17–27 —

17

PROTECTED FROM THE ACCUSER

How do you handle criticism? How does one protect himself from the **"scourge of the tongue"** (Job 5:21)? Where is the Place of Immunity from accusation? If you are going to be successful in the Lord's work, you must find God's hiding place from one of the most painful weapons in Satan's arsenal: the critical tongue.

The fact is, for better or for worse, people are going to talk about you. You cannot do the will of God without causing changes, and changes will always cause some to stumble. In fact, Jesus said we were to beware when all men speak well of us. He said we cannot serve two masters; if we are to truly please Him, we cannot be distracted by trying to please everyone else.

At the same time, there is a demonic strategy that is set against those who teach God's word and minister to His people. The enemy's campaign is not only aimed at destroying the shepherd; he also seeks to scatter the sheep. If Satan's attack is successful, everyone involved will come out of the battle with less love and a hardened heart.

I find it amazing that individuals can react so differently to the same teaching. One will be uplifted and encouraged while another may not only miss the Lord's blessing but actually be offended by an isolated statement.

It seems that for every person who takes the hammer and chisel to make an idol of a preacher, there is someone else with a hammer and spikes ready to crucify him. And unless that man is sustained by the Lord, the pressures against him can be overwhelming.

Most people fail to remember that a minister is just like any other Christian. He is not a superman; bullets (and words) do not bounce off his chest. He is not invulnerable to cruel and malicious talk. He is an imperfect person called to serve the living God in the body of Christ, but just a person, nonetheless.

For most, church is a place people go to express their worship of God, to be taught and to have fellowship. But to the man or woman of God, the church is God's garden. Most of the real work a pastor does is not in the pulpit but in the unheralded service of cultivating love and trust in personal relationships.

In God's eyes, the church is much more than a meeting place of casual acquaintances or doctrinally united believers. To the Father, the church is a living temple, a human house for the Spirit of His Son. The Bible says that when He placed us in our particular church, it actually gave Him pleasure (1 Cor. 12:18). Together with the Holy Spirit, the pastor and elders work to bring the church into a right relationship with God's love and then spread that love throughout the entire citywide church.

God has provided honorable ways for people to transfer from one church to another. If someone wants to leave a church to start their own, there are proper ways to receive God's anointing and be sent (see Acts 13:1–3). It is not necessary to find fault and cause a church split. When things are done correctly and in order, people are edified.

But when relationships are severed and destroyed through malicious gossip, or when a developing trust is turned into mistrust through backbiting and criticism, God Himself is angered (Prov. 6:16–19). And if God is offended, how much more difficult is it for His servant to remain aloof from the conflict that sin causes.

THE ANSWER!

So, how does a man or woman of God find the balance between his basic need to survive and his responsibility to please God? The answer, in a word, is to put on Christ's love.

A number of years ago, I went through a difficult time in which a handful of people made me the target of ongoing criticism. There is a type of constructive criticism coming through people who love you which teaches and helps you to prosper, and there is a type of criticism that comes through an embittered spirit that is not meant to correct you but to destroy you. It was the latter relationship that I had with these people.

To be honest, I am sure that there were areas in my life which were imbalanced; some of their complaints were justified. However, much of what they had to say was said to others behind my back. Our congregation was being destabilized by these individuals. Try as I did, nothing I could say or repent of would silence them.

For three years I sought the Lord, yet He would not vindicate me of their accusations. Instead, He dealt with *me*. He reached deep into the very substructure of my soul and began to touch hidden areas of my life.

At issue with the Lord was not my sin, but my "self." The Bible says that our sins are ever before us (Psalm 51); these I could see. But I had no perspective on my own soul. The Lord allowed this criticism to continue until it unearthed something deeper and more fundamentally wrong than any of my doctrinal interpretations or sins. It unearthed *me*.

The Holy Spirit began to show me how easily I was manipulated by people's criticisms and especially how much my sense of peace was governed by the acceptance or rejection of man. As much as I prayed, God would not deliver me from my enemy. He saved me by *killing* that part of me that was vulnerable to the devil, and He did it with the accusations themselves.

I will never forget the day it dawned on me that both God and the devil wanted me to die, but for different reasons. Satan wanted to destroy me through slander and then drain me with the unceasing activity of explaining "my side" to people. At the same time, God wanted to crucify that part of my soul that was so easily exploited by the devil in the first place!

It was a pivotal day when I realized that this battle was not going to be over until I died to what people said about me. It was probably at this point that I finally and truly became a servant of God.

Today, I stand in awe of what the Lord did during those terrible, yet wonderful, months. He knew a time would come when the things I wrote would touch the lives of millions of people. To inoculate me from the *praise* of man, He baptized me in the *criticism* of man until I died to the control of man.

Do not misunderstand me: I still honestly pray about things submitted to me by others, and I am accountable to other leaders. I even have staff people whose assignment is to give me a critical analysis of my life and work. But I am no longer ruled by man. I live for God's pleasure and if I happen to please man, that is His business, not mine.

THE SHELTER OF HIS CROSS

There is something utterly marvelous about the Lord's redemptive powers. No matter what hardship, devilish plot or accusation is hurled our way, everything Satan would use to destroy is redeemed by God's love and then used to perfect us. If we faithfully seek the Lord, adversity becomes like gasoline upon our heart's fire for God. Just to survive, we are driven deeper into the blaze of His Presence.

Thus, as much as I hated it when people slandered me, this was the very thing God used to compel me nearer to His heart. As important as Bible study and church attendance is, it was *adversity* which worked the deepest death of self and brought me closest to God! I have come to sincerely love and appreciate my enemies—*I could not have come to this place of blessedness without them!*

I can see why Jesus said, "**Blessed are those who have been persecuted for the sake of righteousness. . . for theirs is the kingdom of heaven**" (Matt. 5:10). Certainly, He does not mean that outwardly we experience "**heaven**" when we are persecuted or suffer mental or physical abuse. No, but *inwardly* God deals mightily with our soul, breaking its addiction to man's approval and liberating us to truly live for Christ.

In His wisdom, God gives us two gifts: a new nature and a cross uniquely designed to kill our old nature. *The moment we begin to pick up the cross, we enter the Place of Immunity.*

We must learn this truth: God does not want our old nature to survive. He does not want us to reform that which actually needs to be crucified; He wants it to die. Not only was our old nature corrupt and indefensible against the enemy, but the flesh is akin to the devil and most easily inhabited by him.

The character of the "new nature," however, is Christ Himself. With the living Christ within me, how shall I bring a charge against my neighbor, for Christ commands me to love. If I issue a complaint, shall I raise my old nature from the dead to be my witness? Shall I silence Christ to hear the voice of the accuser? You see, if I am to be the Lord's servant, when offended I must repeat Christ's prayer of the cross, **"Father, forgive them; for they do not know what they are doing"** (Luke 23:34).

So, regardless of man's opinions about us, whether we are exalted or abased, let us determine to carry Christ's cross through the conflict. For these momentary light afflictions are producing for us an eternal weight of glory far beyond all comparison.

My personal attitude is this: I will stand for revival, unity and prayer; I will labor to restore healing and reconciliation between God's people. Yet, if all God truly wanted was to raise up one fully yielded son—a son who would refuse to be offended, refuse to react, refuse to harbor unforgiveness regardless of those who slander and persecute—I have determined to be that person. My primary goal in all things is not revival, but to bring pleasure to Christ.

None of us are there yet, but if we each have this attitude, we will put to death our reactions to criticisms and offenses.

And though we may still stumble, we will learn that carrying the cross is not merely dying to self; it is embracing the love of Christ that forgives the very ones who have crucified you.

Lord, help me to hear with humility the criticisms of those who accuse me. Grant me peace to spiritually prosper when others find fault. Yet, even more than this, help me to die to all I was and live to all You are. I desperately want to be found in Your nature and to be changed into Your image. Amen.

WHOM SHALL I FEAR?

THE LORD IS MY LIGHT AND MY SALVATION;
WHOM SHALL I FEAR?
THE LORD IS THE DEFENSE OF MY LIFE;
WHOM SHALL I DREAD?
WHEN EVILDOERS CAME UPON ME
TO DEVOUR MY FLESH,
MY ADVERSARIES AND MY ENEMIES,
THEY STUMBLED AND FELL.
THOUGH A HOST ENCAMP AGAINST ME,
MY HEART WILL NOT FEAR;
THOUGH WAR ARISE AGAINST ME,
IN SPITE OF THIS I SHALL BE CONFIDENT.

ONE THING I HAVE ASKED FROM THE LORD,
THAT I SHALL SEEK:
THAT I MAY DWELL IN THE HOUSE OF THE LORD
ALL THE DAYS OF MY LIFE,
TO BEHOLD THE BEAUTY OF THE LORD,
AND TO MEDITATE IN HIS TEMPLE.
FOR IN THE DAY OF TROUBLE
HE WILL CONCEAL ME IN HIS TABERNACLE;
IN THE SECRET PLACE OF HIS TENT
HE WILL HIDE ME;
HE WILL LIFT ME UP ON A ROCK.

— PSALM 27:1–5 —

18

AT THE THRONE
WITH GOD

BIRTHING THE PROMISE OF GOD

There is a time when, having been touched by God, something truly of Christ is conceived in your spirit. It is actually a time when the hopes of God begin to fill your imagination and dreams. The experience is very much like a pregnancy. That which God has conceived within you is now being nurtured by your faith and protected through your prayers. Christ is being formed within you (Gal. 4:19). From this time on, your walk with God is never merely a religion—it is a destiny.

Yet, at this stage of our development, spiritual immaturity is unavoidable. It takes time for the promise of God to gestate within us. We struggle with impatience and anxiety. We think that, on our own initiative, we can attain all that God has promised. If we accept delays, we are harassed by guilt.

It takes time before we finally realize that only God can fulfill what He has promised. Our task is to cooperate with Him in the preparation of our hearts. Thus, the first stages of our walk with Christ are usually not times of fulfillment but development.

But the Almighty is not the only supernatural personality intently watching our lives. Satan also senses the sacredness and destiny of the life that is growing within us. Especially as our time of fulfillment actually draws near, the devil seeks to abort the work of God within us. We face battles inside and out. In the dark hours of the night we question our motives and doubt our readiness.

Externally, we face accusations of the people Satan uses to accuse or criticize our actions. We react wrongly to those whose attitudes Satan manipulates. We argue our case before them—*Something of God is in me! Don't you see? Don't criticize, help me!*

Yet, rarely do we find comfort seeking the approval of men, and what comfort we find is fleeting. Shall we blame men for their apparent lack of support? No. For by divine decree, no one can truly supply us with the support we crave except the Lord Himself. Even though we may owe our very spiritual existence to the intercessory prayer of another, what God conceives within us, ultimately, must find its strength in Christ alone.

You will remember that when Solomon built the temple, he had inscribed upon its two pillars the names *Jachin* and *Boaz* (1 Kings 7:21). *Jachin* meant, "He will establish;" *Boaz* meant, "in Him is strength." If we will enter and abide in true service to God, we must abandon reliance upon any strength but His or any success except what He establishes.

PRAYER BEGETS BREAKTHROUGH

The book of Revelations, chapter 12, provides us an insight into the pattern of true spiritual growth. We see here a depiction of Christ's inception within us. It is followed by the gestation period of preparation and the attempt of Satan to abort the emergence of Christ in our lives. Finally, we see the manifestation of Christ's nature revealed and functional through His human servant.

John saw a great sign, **"A woman clothed with the sun, and the moon under her feet, and on her head a crown of twelve stars; and she was with child"** (Rev. 12:1–2). Various commentators see this woman as Israel birthing Christ or the saints of both covenants becoming the New Israel. Others see the process whereby God moves people to release through prayer great spiritual awakenings among the nations. Still others see a type of the extraordinary intercession of saints at the end of the age, whose travail consummates itself in Christ's return.

Whatever the travailing woman in Revelation, chapter 12, signifies, our primary focus is on the *principle* we see underlying her activity. Mirrored in this woman's pain is the reflection, on a much smaller scale, of our own struggle to truly see Christ birthed in our service to God.

Without minimizing the importance of good works or faithfulness to our current task, there is a time when something deep within us demands we rise to meet our approaching destiny with extraordinary prayer. It is a time when a new dimension of Christ is about to emerge in our lives.

The woman in labor has carried God's purposes to the point of breakthrough. The energy she expended in all her former works fuses into one great labor of prayer: **"she cried out, being in labor and in pain to give birth"** (v. 2). In this deep intercession, she gives birth to one who will **"rule all the nations with a rod of iron"** (v. 5).

So also with us. The vision God has put in our spirit may not rule the entire world, but when it emerges it will be Christ: He will rule *our* world. However, He cannot come forth apart from our faith, preparation and travailing prayer. There is a time to work, serve and be seen. There is another time when the purpose of God within us is at hand. This is a time for focused prayer.

It is significant that in recent years the Lord has led the church into greater, more fervent prayer. There is nothing less noble about the works of the Lord, but a new purpose is about to be born. It is time to pray.

THE ENEMY'S ASSAULT

If all there was to launching a new move of God was prayer, we would, by now, be in revival. But, as John's vision reveals, the woman in Revelation, chapter 12, was about to give birth when there appeared another sign: **"A great red dragon . . . stood before the woman . . . so that when she gave birth he might devour her child. And she gave birth to a son, a male child"** (Rev. 12:3–5).

Most believe this one who was born to the woman represents the person and work of Jesus Christ. Yet, even the Son of God began His life as a baby: small and defenseless. Likewise, everyone whom God has ever used—everything God has ever done since the fall of Adam—has entered the world in a vulnerable condition and in need of protection. It is while the new work of God is trembling forward that Satan seeks to bring his greatest assault. The form he takes in his war against our new beginnings in Christ is accusation.

It is during this time that God's purpose for us is most vulnerable. The dragon that positioned itself at the womb of the woman is, in the same chapter, revealed as the devil, specifically identified as the accuser of the brethren.

THE POWER OF WORDS

When the devil accuses you, he does not come with accusations that are without some measure of truth. He points out our littleness, emphasizes our lack of spirituality, exploits our ignorance and fears, and condemns us for our immaturity and failures. Using mere words, he halts, or at least hinders, our new beginnings.

Recall your first witness to someone about Christ or perhaps the first time you spoke in a Bible study. For many, a flood of words stormed against their heart afterwards. Those words came from the accuser of the brethren.

Because of this spirit, the purpose of God in many Christians has been aborted. Many who ought to be in awe of the Spirit of Christ within them have settled instead for a mere theology about Jesus Christ. Thus, Satan exploited their imperfections and buried their hope of Christ under a barrage of accusation.

Even if the accuser has successfully hindered *you* in this regard, know this with certainty: *Christ in you cannot die.* He only awaits a new mixture of hope with faith, and prayer with perseverance. The enemy you are fighting is not failure, ignorance, or lack of spirituality; your enemy is the accuser of the brethren. He seeks to manipulate your shortcomings and use them against you. Through a flood of words, he wants to reduce your relationship with God to a hollow religion, void of the reality of Christ's life.

CAUGHT UP TO GOD

How do we overcome this accusing spirit, this devil that seeks to stop the revelation of Christ in our lives? Let us return to the twelfth chapter of Revelations where we find the key which unlocks our destiny in God. **"And she gave birth to a son, a male child, who is to rule all the nations with a rod of iron; and her child was caught up to God and to His throne"** (Rev. 12:5). As the woman's child **"was caught up to God and to His throne,"** so also must we be "caught up," abiding in the living Presence of God Himself.

We cannot allow ourselves to be deterred by the devil's accusation or people's opinions. If the weapon of the accuser is words, know also that our victory is God's word. He has said that we are His children—that His Son abides within us, bringing us justification, righteousness, holiness and power.

Since the moment we first came to Christ, there has been an updraft of the Holy Spirit—a constant drawing from God—lifting us upward toward the fulness of His Presence. We have seen for ourselves: all things work together for good. We are convinced by our own experience: nothing can separate us from the love of God in Christ Jesus our Lord (Rom 8:28, 38–39). Let us, therefore, surrender to this wind of God and in adoring obedience allow Him to carry us into our holy future.

It is a most solemn yet joyous truth: *The rapture for which the church awaits has already begun in our spirits!* **Right now, God has "raised us up with Him, and seated us with Him in the heavenly places, in Christ Jesus"!** (Eph. 2:6) Did not Jesus say, **"I am the resurrection and the life"?** (John 11:25) The resurrection, Jesus tells us, is not merely an event; it is a Person—and He is within us today, ever renewing and drawing us upward toward the fulness of God!

Satan's strategy is to keep us carnal, religious and earthbound. But he is too late! For we are, even now, heaven-born and bound for glory. Are we not born again from above? Is it not written that the Jerusalem above is our mother? (Gal. 4:26) Heaven is not merely our destiny; it is our homeland, the place of our birth!

So, our first strategy against the accuser is to refuse to allow *any* words other than the Word of God to define our future. When the accuser attacks, instead of descending to his level of accusation, we must ascend in praise to the height of Christ's exaltation. We flee into the Presence of God.

Yes, in the power of Christ's goodness He redeems even the assault of the accuser of the brethren. For it is the accuser that God uses to trouble us toward higher ground. And our God shall continue to reverse the effects of the devil's accusation until we not only come to the throne of God's grace in our need, but we learn to abide with Christ in heavenly places! This Place of Immunity is the place of our destiny, where we are spiritually caught up to God and His throne.

Master, how I praise You for Your ability to take even what was meant for evil and use it for my good. Thank You for turning the assault of the accuser into a goad to push me toward Your Presence. There is no place I would rather be than secure with You at Your throne. Grant me a humble heart that, even when faced by the accuser, I might quickly flee to You for safety. Amen.

God Is Our Refuge

God is our refuge and strength,
a very present help in trouble.
Therefore we will not fear,
though the earth should change,
and though the mountains
slip into the heart of the sea;
Though its waters roar and foam,
though the mountains quake
at its swelling pride. Selah.

There is a river whose streams
make glad the city of God,
The holy dwelling places of the Most High.
God is in the midst of her,
she will not be moved;
God will help her when morning dawns.
The nations made an uproar,
the kingdoms tottered;
He raised His voice, the earth melted.
The Lord of hosts is with us;
The God of Jacob is our stronghold. Selah.

— Psalm 46:1–7 —

19

ROBED IN HIS GLORY

The Spirit of Christ in heaven is the same Spirit of Christ in us. The difference is, in heaven, Jesus is robed in glory; on earth, He is disguised in our imperfect flesh. But Christ is the same whether in heaven or in us.

Paul makes the source of power and glory in the church very clear. He said: "Test yourselves to see if you are in the faith; examine yourselves! Or do you not recognize this about yourselves, that Jesus Christ is in you—unless indeed you fail the test?" (2 Cor. 13:5)

In another place Paul defined his inner spiritual life as being "crucified with Christ." He continued: "It is no longer I who live, but Christ lives in me; and the life which I now live in the flesh I live by faith in the Son of

God, who loved me and delivered Himself up for me. I do not nullify the grace of God" (Gal. 2:20).

What is this grace of God? The old, sinful self-life we once knew is crucified so that Christ Himself might bring His glory to us. From the beginning, to make man in His image has been the unwavering purpose of God. There is no other plan. God shall consummate this plan as the age ends. In Revelation 10:7, we read, **"In the days of the voice of the seventh angel, when he is about to sound, then the mystery of God is finished."** What is this "mystery of God"? The mystery of God is **"Christ in you, the hope of glory"** (Col. 1:27).

You see, a time is coming when the mystery of God shall be a mystery no more. Our time of preparation shall be complete and we shall be like Him. Our corruptible, mortal lives shall put on incorruption; we shall wear immortality like a shining garment. As Christ robed Himself in our imperfect flesh, so shall we be robed in His resplendent glory.

Thus, our holy objective is to make way in our hearts for the coming of the Lord. With the vision of God's glory, we pick up our cross, knowing that the sufferings of this present age are themselves being used by God to produce in us an eternal weight of glory far beyond all comparisons!

Paul wrote,

[We are] **always carrying about in the body the dying of Jesus, that the life of Jesus also may be manifested in our body. For we who live are constantly being delivered over to death for Jesus' sake, that the life of Jesus also may be manifested in our mortal flesh.** —2 Corinthians 4:10–11

The life of Jesus—He is our goal and glory! **"And it was for this He called you through our gospel, that you may gain the glory of our Lord Jesus Christ"** (2 Thess. 2:14). Indeed, He is coming **"to be glorified in His saints on that day, and to be marveled at among all who have believed"** (2 Thess. 1:10). **"For you have died and your life is hidden with Christ in God. When Christ, who is our life, is revealed, then you also will be revealed with Him in glory"** (Col. 3:3–4). It is this life, the life of Christ, which is the Place of Immunity.

This is not some "deep teaching," this is basic Christianity! We are "living epistles," known and read by all men. The church is to be the revelation of Jesus Christ that the world sees! Did not Jesus Himself say, **"Father, I desire that they also, whom Thou hast given Me, be with Me where I am, in order that they may behold My glory"**? (John 17:24)

Yet, to behold His glory is but the first stage of receiving His very glory into our lives. He also said:

> **And the glory which Thou hast given Me I have given to them; that they may be one, just as We are one. I in them, and Thou in Me, that they may be perfected in unity, that the world may know that Thou didst send Me, and didst love them, even as Thou didst love Me.**   —John 17:22–23

Our goal is not to tell the world about Christianity but to reveal the glory of Christ. We are not called to imitate Jesus in detached obedience but to actually let Him shine through us to mankind.

Right now, there are two persons within every Christian: Jesus and self. Each of us must learn to dwell in Him. **"In that day,"** Jesus said, **"you shall know that I am in My Father, and you in Me, and I in you"** (John 14:20).

A day is coming, and now is, when the most important truth you can know is that you are in Christ and Christ is in you. **"If anyone loves Me, he will keep My word; and My Father will love him, and We will come to him, and make Our abode with him"** (John 14:23). Our life, once full of rebellion and self-interest, has been set apart to become the abode of God, the dwelling of God in glory.

TO BE KNOWN FOR KNOWING HIM

In our immaturity, we have sought to be known for many things. We sought to make a name for ourselves through our spiritual gifts or doctrinal emphasis. Some sought renown for their type of church government; others desired recognition through a building or evangelistic program.

Today, if we seek renown it must be for this alone: *to be known for knowing Christ.* His promise is that His Presence, His very Spirit and power, will uninhibitedly accompany those who follow only Him.

Thus, our focus must be upon Christ alone, for through Him God will ultimately accompany their lives with great glory. Yes, great signs and wonders will increasingly flow from our hands, but the miraculous will not distract our gaze from Jesus. For we are not seeking the power of God, but the *Person* of God. When our hands are not being laid upon the sick, they will be lifted up in worship.

Thus, we find the Holy Spirit directing us continually back to Jesus. Without Him, our prayers are just rituals. Apart from Him, our Christianity can do nothing. But *with* Him we enter a shelter of glory; in His Presence we find the Place of Immunity.

THE CANOPY OF GLORY

"The Lord will create over the whole area of Mount Zion and over her assemblies a cloud by day, even smoke, and the brightness of a flaming fire by night; for over all the glory will be a canopy" (Isa. 4:5). There is a glory coming that shall be a source of protection for the saints. "And there will be a shelter to give shade from the heat by day, and refuge and protection from the storm and the rain" (v. 6).

How does this glory come? God is leading the church into a baptism of fire. He has purposed to wash away the "filth of the daughters of Zion," He has set His heart to purge the "bloodshed of Jerusalem from her midst, by the spirit of judgment and the spirit of burning" (Isa. 4:4). The purer we become, the greater the glory that shall shine through us, and the greater the glory, the more spacious the Place of Immunity.

Lord, to know You in Your glory is to dwell forever in the Place of Immunity. But to know Your glory, I must renounce the "glory" of myself, my denomination and my culture. You are my glory and the lifter of my head. Baptize me in the light of Your splendor; grant me the grace You granted Moses: a tent of meeting where I may behold Your radiance and beauty. Clothe me in Your Presence and I shall ask for nothing more.

His Glory Will
Appear Upon You

Arise, shine; for your light has come,
And the glory of the Lord
has risen upon you.
For behold, darkness will cover the earth,
And deep darkness the peoples;

But the Lord will rise upon you,
And His glory will appear upon you.
And nations will come to your light,
And kings to the brightness of your rising.

— Isaiah 60:1–3 —

20

IN GOD'S
TABERNACLE

We began this book warning about the pressures and battles that confront us in our world today. Our hope is that we have by now found our supply of strength and Place of Immunity in God alone. Yet, Jesus also warned of the deception which would occur at the end of the age. When we consider His words, we instinctively think of false teachers and prophets; and these will, indeed, mislead many (see Matthew 24).

But there is another dimension to the enemy's tactics that is, perhaps, even more dangerous. For we may actually know the truth but be too preoccupied and distracted to obey it. If this is the case, greater judgment will fall on us than upon him who did not know God's will at all.

Jesus warned, **"Be on guard, that your hearts may not be weighted down with dissipation and drunkenness and the worries of life, and that day come on you suddenly like a trap"** (Luke 21:34).

To *dissipate* means "to fritter away; employ aimlessly; squander; be wasteful." Besides giving us His grace, the second most important gift Christ has given us is time. If we do not have time, we cannot develop spiritually in any of God's other gifts or resources. If we fail to *make* time for the service of God, we will be unprepared for this day which, Jesus said, **"will come upon all those who dwell on the face of all the earth"** (Luke 21:35). The day of the Lord will not be an occasion of joy; it will come upon you like a trap.

Over and again the Lord warned that those who put Him off now will be put off by Him later (see 24:36–25:46; Luke 13:24–30; John 12:47–48). They will seek His protection, but He will not provide it. Why? It takes time to grow in the ways, knowledge and grace of God, and it is this very growth which creates within us access to the Place of Immunity. Today is the day to prepare for tomorrow; to wait for tomorrow to ready ourselves will be too late.

IN THE INNER COURT

In the book of Revelations there is a marvel. John writes, **"And there was given me a measuring rod like a staff; and someone said, 'Rise and measure the temple of God, and the altar, and those who worship in it'** (Rev. 11:1). John was commanded to measure the **"temple of God."** When John's vision came, it should be noted that the physical temple in Jerusalem had been reduced to rubble for over twenty years. The apostle was not commanded to measure the *physical* temple but the *spiritual* temple. The church is the spiritual temple.

He was told to measure the altar and those who worship in it. In other words, he was commanded to *measure those who have presented themselves as living sacrifices to God.* These are the souls who have poured out their lives upon the altar of sacrifice (Phil. 2:17); they have learned the secret of abiding in the holy place with God.

John also was told, **"Leave out the court which is outside the temple, and do not measure it, for it has been given to the nations; and they will tread under foot the holy city for forty-two months"** (Rev. 11:2).

There are three distinct groups identified to John in this vision: those who worship at God's altar, those immediately outside the temple, and the nations that will tread underfoot the holy city for 3½ years. The **"nations,"** in this context, represent those who shall persecute the unprepared church, which was in the court **"outside the temple."** Those who worship at the altar are those who, through love and perseverance, dwell in the Place of Immunity at the end of the age.

NEITHER MALE NOR FEMALE, BUT CHRIST

The court that was outside the temple was actually part of the temple grounds and was contained within the wall surrounding the entire temple enclosure. It was called the **"court of women and gentiles."** Only the priests, who were male in gender, could serve in the inner courts of God.

This does not mean that, today, women cannot enter the Holy Place; it means women must become "sons." To overcome they must crucify reliance upon seduction and manipulation; they must ascend higher than the limitations of jealousy and fear. All of these things must go to the cross, so that God's one Son, Christ, might come forth in their lives in the true beauty of holiness.

Before the men of the church consider themselves falsely secure, we are not saying women must become like men. No! God forbid! For men also must repent of their rebellion to God, their spiritual irresponsibility and the multitude of ways men express their carnality in games and ambitions and desires for control.

A "son," Paul says, "is neither male nor female" (Gal. 3:28). God's sons are individuals who have literally "clothed [themselves] with Christ" (v. 27). They are fully submitted to Him as their source of identification. They are bold yet meek, free yet slaves, uncompromising in vision yet tolerant toward the weak. To leave the "court of women and gentiles," regardless of one's gender, we all must leave the deception of our flesh nature and enter the Presence of God. In our spirits, we must become "a holy temple in the Lord ... a dwelling of God in the Spirit" (Eph. 2:21–22).

In the last moments of this age, there will be those who, although they live on earth, consciously dwell in the tabernacle of God in heaven. They have made the Person of Christ their treasure; where their treasure is, there their heart is also (Matt. 6:21).

And, as the age concludes, there will be those who profess Christianity but have never truly taken Christ's commandments, promises and warnings seriously. When the times of judgment come, they will be found unprepared for God.

I would fail in my service to Christ if I did not warn you of the Master's return and the purity and preparation He requires of His church. Yet, He also gives us His unfailing promise: a place of protection, high and secure, full of spiritual authority and graced with power. The Place of

Immunity is the Presence of God; it is found at God's altar by those who worship in it.

Lord, how easily distracted I am, how dissipated by the things of this age. Master, I want one thing: to dwell in Your house all the days of my life, to behold the beauty of the Lord and meditate in Your temple.

This day I choose to ascend in worship to Your throne. This day I determine to live in view of Your glory. Joyfully, I enter the Place of Immunity with You. Amen.

In Conclusion

It is with reluctance that I conclude this first portion of our two-book set. I say "reluctance" because the Bible is brimming with promises of divine protection. What I have provided here is barely an outline. Study for yourself the promises God brings to those who fear Him, or to those who walk uprightly with humility and wisdom.

In the second book of this series we shall take a more militant stand. Our prayer will become persevering, our discernment of the enemy sharper. But it is from this glorious stronghold, the Place of Immunity, that we advance. For it is here that we have learned to clothe ourselves with Christ, and Christ is the full armor of God. He is our Place of Immunity.